The MBO Guide for Management Teams

CW00553658

By Andy Nash

HARRIMAN HOUSE LTD

43 Chapel Street
Petersfield
Hampshire
GU32 3DY
GREAT BRITAIN

Tel: +44 (0)1730 233870
Fax: +44 (0)1730 233880
Email: enquiries@harriman-house.com
Website: www.harriman-house.com

First published in Great Britain in 2005

Published by Harriman House Ltd

The right of Andy Nash to be identified as the author has been asserted
in accordance with the Copyright, Design and Patents Act 1988.

ISBN 1-897-59751-7

British Library Cataloguing in Publication Data
A CIP catalogue record for this book can be obtained from the British Library.

All rights reserved; no part of this publication may be reproduced, stored in a retrieval
system, or transmitted in any form or by any means, electronic, mechanical,
photocopying, recording, or otherwise without the prior written permission of the
Publisher. This book may not be lent, resold, hired out or otherwise disposed of by
way of trade in any form of binding or cover other than that in which it is published
without the prior written consent of the Publisher.

Printed and bound by Ashford Colour Press Ltd, Gosport, Hampshire.

No responsibility for loss occasioned to any person or corporate body acting or
refraining to act as a result of reading material in this book can be accepted by the
Publisher, by the Author, or by the employer of the Author.

For Linda, Olivia, Edward, Virginia & Imogen

and

To all those in MBOs trying to make their dreams come true.

About the Author

Andy Nash is probably best known as a key member of the management team that bought out Taunton Cider for £72.5m in 1991, floated it the following year for £153m and sold it three years later for £280m.

Since then, as a portfolio chairman, he has been brought in to grapple with a string of MBOs/MBIs in various states of financial health and has achieved many notable corporate successes.

He has also been chairman of two publicly-quoted companies, the drinks company Merrydown and the security business Photo-Scan. Both have found new owners recently, and both sets of shareholders have been paid a handsome premium.

Soon after joining Merrydown as chairman in 1997, Andy reformulated the board and brought in a new CEO. They initiated a new corporate strategy, substantially rationalising and simplifying the business. This enabled a refinancing to take place and losses were quickly replaced by profits. When Andy joined the business its market value was just £2.5m; Merrydown has now been sold for £37m.

Andy has also served as a non-executive director for the City law firm Kirkpatrick & Lockhart Nicholson Graham since 1998.

For good measure the 47-year old, who hails from Cheddon Fitzpaine in Somerset, is partial to the game of cricket and fits in time to be deputy chairman of Somerset County Cricket Club.

If you are considering an MBO/MBI, or are presently managing one, and you think Andy may be able to help you, don't hesitate to contact him.

mbombi@btinternet.com

www.mbombi.com

Acknowledgements

Andy Burrows and Mike Wright at the CMBOR at Nottingham University for invaluable research information and advice.

Mike Molesworth for the Dennis-Eagle Ltd story.

Malcolm Howell for assistance on the Cloverleaf story.

Patrick Dunne at 3i for his support and ideas.

Peter Lee and Nigel Skinner for their help with the Tubex Ltd story.

Nick Kerton for his help on the Maybridge story.

Jeff Bocan for helping out on the Ashford Colour Press Ltd section.

Marc Garrido and his team at the SAS Radisson for all their help and assistance.

Robin Tutty at Kirkpatrick & Lockhart Nicholson Graham for advice and information.

John Mackie of the British Venture Capital Association for his encouragement and support.

Graham Spooner for his sage advice.

John Rudofsky for his comments and assistance on the manuscript.

Myles and Stephen at Harriman House for encouragement and fixing all the mistakes.

The team at Ashford Colour Press for printing the book itself.

Contents

Introduction

The book is aimed at prospective and existing managers of a management buy-out or management buy-in. MBOs/MBIs are inherently risky with the failure rate being relatively high. This book can increase your chances of success, by describing some common elephant traps, bad practices and risks, and how best to avoid them.

MBOs/MBIs make or lose fortunes for the risk-takers because of the leverage involved. Leverage is the fulcrum on which these deals see-saw between success and failure. Every venture capitalist's portfolio has a range of leveraged companies, and average returns to their investors are determined by the balance between their star investments and those which stagnate or go bust. Leverage is a business school type of word – my eldest daughter would probably say it was cool! If your company were a car, leveraging it is like filling the boot with high explosive, and then driving off on a long journey with your fingers crossed.

Management buy-outs and buy-ins are a hi-octane part of the business world. Since 2001, the most common exit for MBOs/MBIs hasn't been flotation, or even trade sales, but receivership. It is a high-risk/reward arena. Metaphorically, an MBO/MBI is like fitting an 8 litre V12 engine into an aged VW Beetle and expecting it to perform much better than before, or as someone more colourfully put it: a venture capitalist would expect that if you made love nine times in a night, the baby will arrive in four weeks.

Since 1991 I have been involved with eight such deals. They vary greatly: from staggering success to the verge of financial oblivion – and fortunately back again. The deals have ranged across very different markets; from the sophisticated world of global drug discovery in mythical Tintagel, to heavy metal bashing (dustcarts) in the West Midlands. The deals have been backed by many different venture capitalists, and financed by UK and international banks.

I have carried out a variety of roles across these deals: chairman, executive director, non-executive director and as a personal coach to a managing director. I have been very fortunate to have seen many MBOs/MBIs through the prism of management, and have drawn on the experience to write this book. I have also attempted to make what can be a serious and turgid subject easy-reading, and on occasions perhaps almost entertaining!

Chapter 1

The Market
and some Basic Principles

The Venture Capital Market

History in the UK

The genesis of venture capital in the UK can be traced back to the great crash of public stock markets in 1929. The Macmillan Report in 1931 highlighted the equity gap which was a constraining factor in the recovery and growth of companies. This ultimately led to the creation of two organisations: the *Industrial and Commercial Finance Corporation* and the Finance Corporation for Industry. In the 1980s these merged to form what is now 3i plc.

Since 1983 (when records began), members of the British Venture Capital Association have invested an aggregate sum well in excess of £60bn in more than 25,000 companies. This contribution to the UK's economic effort cannot be over-stated. Many companies who might otherwise have languished, or even disappeared completely, have achieved growth and prosperity.

Some explanations and definitions

The venture capital industry has evolved into three main areas:

1. *Venture Capital* for **early-stage investment**. This is also referred to as *start-up capital, seed capital* or *boot-strap funding*.
2. *Development Capital* for **emerging businesses**, which have grown beyond the start-up phase.
3. *Private Equity* funding for **mature businesses.**

The practitioners, however, tend to be referred to generically as *venture capitalists*.

Investments by venture capitalist organisations have historically been concentrated in unquoted companies. In recent years investments in public companies (public-private or P2P's) have become more common, as some boards have opted to leave the increasingly demanding and unforgiving arena of the London Stock Exchange's Main Market.

Rather like air under pressure, equity invested by venture capitalist organisations always seeks an exit, usually by sale to another trade party, or occasionally via flotation. That said, the most common exit for MBOs/MBIs since 2001 has unfortunately been receivership – but more on that later. First, a few term definitions.

- *MBO*

  Management buy-out. This is typically where an existing management team buys the company in which they work from the shareholder(s).

- *IBO*

  An institutional buy-out. An institution will acquire a company and incentivise a management team to run it for them.

- *MBI*

  Management buy-in. A new management team acquires a business from shareholder(s) and replaces the incumbent management.

- *BIMBO*

  A combination of an MBO/MBI. An existing management team is joined by at least one new manager as it acquires the company.

- *VIMBO*

  A vendor initiated MBO, where the owner encourages and facilitates the management team taking ownership of the company.

Market size

The venture capital market is mind-bogglingly large. The British Venture Capital Association (BVCA) has around 165 full members, which comprises the vast majority of UK based firms in this market place. These firms are invested in companies who in total employ nearly three million people in the UK alone. That is equivalent to some 18% of the private sector workforce. The venture capital industry invests in virtually every known sector of the economy across the country.

In addition, the UK accounts for about 40% of the whole of the European market; globally, only the market in the United States is bigger.

Companies in the venture capitalists' sweet-spot

From the buffet of companies always on offer, venture capital investors seek businesses which are well-run, with sound growth prospects, and sustainable competitive advantages in their markets. The more adventurous venture capitalists will also seek out under-managed businesses which, perhaps with the grafting of new members on to the present management team, they believe can be run more successfully.

The quality of the management team in an MBO/MBI is paramount. The team must inspire confidence and have a sustained track record of achievement in business. Investors will go to considerable lengths to verify their initial perceptions of the management team. Additionally the management team must demonstrate strong commitment (underpinned by personal investment), and tangible confidence in their business plan and the future prospects of their company.

Management teams' rewards will be directly linked to their ability to increase profits and, in the fullness of time, succeed in achieving an exit, which crystallises value.

What do the venture capitalists bring to the party?

Venture capitalists are first and foremost a source of finance. However, they can add value to businesses in a number of different ways:

- strategic and other skills complementary to those of the management team;
- additional management resources e.g. non-executive directors;
- business judgement acquired from a considerable breadth of experience;
- personal contacts and networks;
- support identifying, and negotiating with other, fund-providers (e.g. banks);
- mergers and acquisitions experience; and
- exit planning and achievement.

While it is unusual for venture capitalist investors to become involved in day-to-day management decisions, they will stay close to the business and expect to be consulted on all significant decisions, and informed of any major developments – positive or negative. This is often achieved with a seat on the board (they often have the right to appoint an independent non-executive director). The breadth of experience they bring to bear is usually of considerable value to any business, in particular for a company carrying an inherently unstable cargo of debt.

Performance of the venture capital sector

The figures speak for themselves. Taken over the long-term, companies backed by venture capital have significantly out-performed public companies. The reasons for this probably merit a separate study, which I shall not attempt here!

However, the results are a fine advertisement for the sheer hard work, effort and ingenuity put in by the venture capitalists and their management teams. As a wise man once said: "the harder I work, the luckier I get".

Figure 1.1: UK private equity performance

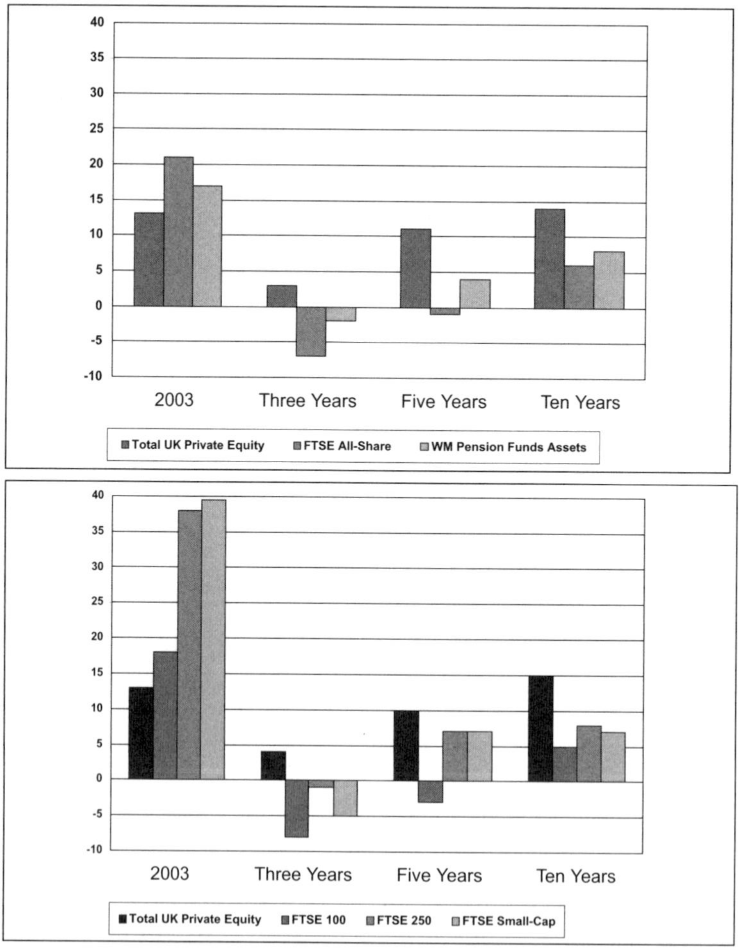

Source: British Venture Capital Association

Why do a deal?

The right answer to this, or at least the one your backers will want to hear, is because you want to make money, since if you do, then so do they. That's the easy bit: now how do these deals come about?

There are some truly wonderful and elegant stories of how management teams of gifted individuals, researched, targeted, approached, negotiated, and closed the perfect deal. Some of these, within no time at all, might also have sold-out and sailed off into the horizon, fulfilled and financially secure for life.

This hasn't always been my experience! The conception of my first MBO was, oddly enough, at a gents' urinal, in Suffolk. The Taunton Cider board meeting was being held at Copella Ltd, which we had recently acquired, and Peter Adams (Taunton Cider's managing director) informed yours truly that, "You can forget the new incentive scheme Nasher [that's me], Tony Portno [Bass plc's main board director] has just told me we are up for sale". You can picture the scene! I didn't know it then but that is where the Taunton Cider MBO was conceived. No sooner had Peter Adams dried his hands then he was off on a mission!

I believe many MBOs and MBIs begin in such a random fashion. The trick for management teams is to spot the opportunity, and then know how to exploit it.

Are you sure you really want to do a deal?

This is a question worthy of the most serious soul-searching. Whether your first deal is conceived at a gents' urinal, as happened in my case, or in lecture room 3b at Harvard Business School, you need to focus on this. You are well-advised to pause for serious thought before embarking on such a white-knuckle ride which, if it goes pear-shaped, could ruin your finances and career.

Rags or riches?

Bluntly, if your deal works out well, and you achieve a successful exit, you will have reached a land of milk and honey. You will have achieved partial or total financial independence. You could burn your suit, play golf all day, do that world tour, and write that novel maybe. Fantastic!

On the other hand, if you fail, you will probably do so slowly, and in front of a lot of people, and financially you will probably be substantially worse off than before. Your professional and personal reputation may also be stained – perhaps in tatters. In short, in doing an MBO/MBI you will be betting your career, and your wealth, on it.

Quite often it seems a team is featured in the broadsheets having made millions from the flotation or sale of their company. Less often do you see the photos – thin watery smiles all round – of those who blew it!

Pressure

As anyone who has completed an MBO/MBI will tell you, they have probably never worked so hard in their professional lives. The work load, combined with jack-hammer stress levels, means this is not a journey for the faint-hearted.

The essential problem is that to produce a business plan, which is of a quality to bear scrutiny of the type a venture capitalist will give it, takes time – a *lot* of time. You will have to sell this plan, and all its consequences, to many other parties, most of them will be world-class in healthy scepticism and sussing you out. You also have to find the time to do this in addition to your current job – which is unlikely to be part-time.

Persistence

One quality you will need above all is persistence.

> *"Nothing in the world can take the place of persistence.*
> *Talent will not: nothing is more common than unsuccessful men with talent.*
> *Genius will not: unrewarded genius is almost a proverb.*
> *Education will not: the world is full of educated derelicts.*
> *Persistence and determination alone are omnipotent."*
> Chay Blyth.

Individuals and teams will face a real test of their will and character. Things frequently go awry (current trading, competitive actions and arguments with vendors to name but a few) and one needs to be very determined and focused to stay the course.

Home life

Whether your MBO/MBI succeeds or fails, your life will have changed for good. It behoves you to discuss with your family the fact you are minded to bet your career, and possibly most of your assets, on buying a company.

If you emerge from these family discussions with your plan intact, you might also reflect on whether you truly have the support of a stable life behind you before you dance with wolves. If you have a family member who is seriously ill, if your daughter is getting divorced, or if your football team has just been relegated etc. are you really in the right frame of mind to do this deal? Think very, very carefully before you commit yourself. If in doubt – take advice.

How does an MBO/MBI work?

There are many books and articles which explain this very competently (please refer to the *Recommended reading* at the back of the book). I would recommend the accountants among you to read a detailed version of how they work. My version below is rather simple, but the principles apply to most deals.

Table 1.1: Simple MBO example

	2000 MBO (£m)	2004 Exit (£m)
Sales	10	15
Costs	9	13
EBIT	1	2
PER	10	10
Company value	10	20
Senior debt	7	5
Equity	3	15
Preference shares	2.5	1.5
Sweet equity value	0.5	13.5
Sweet equity – Institution	75% (i.e. 375k)	75% i.e. 10.125m
Sweet equity – Management	25% (i.e. 125k)	25% i.e. 3.375m

Notes

- In the four year period, sales have increased by 50% to £15m.

- Costs have increased at a lesser rate, causing profit at the earnings before interest and tax level (EBIT) to double to £2m.

- Applying the same price-earnings ratio of 10, company value has doubled to £20m.

- Senior debt, due to repayments, stands at £5m, so the residual equity value increases from £3m to £15m – a five-fold increase.

- The preference shares, after some redemption payments, are £1.5m, which means the sweet equity has multiplied twenty-seven times. This is the effect of leverage.

- Management often have a 25% stake of the sweet equity, so their initial stake of £125,000 has increased to £3.375m. A very satisfactory return by any measure, and not uncommon for successful MBOs/MBIs.

There are many variations on the example opposite but the key principles hold true. Many MBOs/MBIs have multiplied EBIT several times. You can imagine the effect on the equity value in these deals. However, it should be noted that the formula works just as impressively in reverse; a reduction in profit can wipe out equity value very quickly.

How many deals are done in the UK?

Volume of deals

The *Centre for Management Buy-Out Research* (CMBOR) at Nottingham University Business School, which is funded by Barclays Private Equity and Deloitte, provides very valuable and illuminating information.

Chart 1.1: Trends of buy-outs/buy-ins, 1984-2004

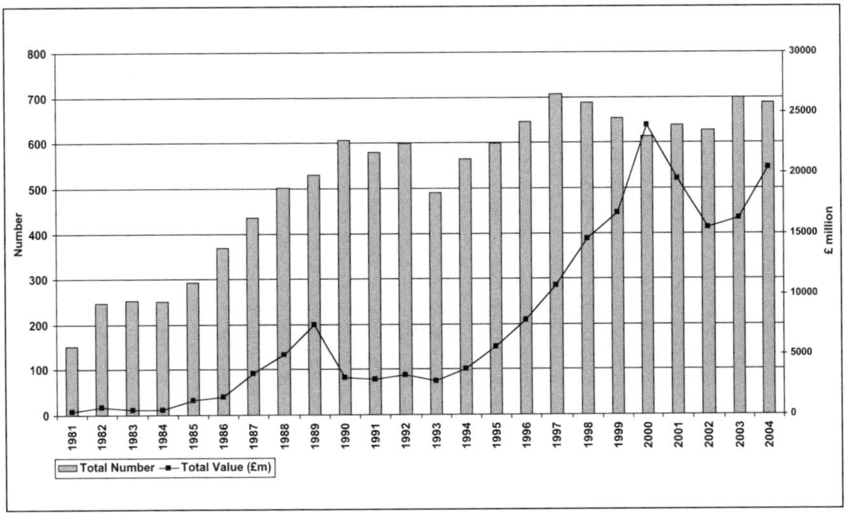

Source: CMBOR/Barclays Private Equity/Deloitte

Notes

- The value of deals peaked at £23.9bn in 2000.

- Annual deal volume has consistently hovered between 600-700 in recent years.

- Average deal value is around £25m.

Chart 1.2: Number of UK buy-outs and buy-ins

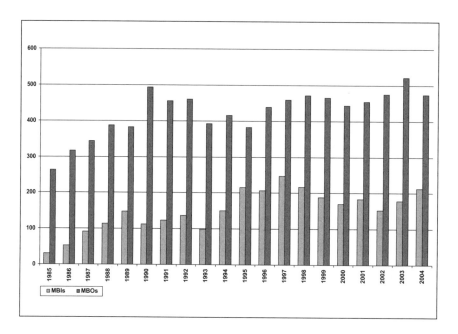

Source: CMBOR/Barclays Private Equity/Deloitte

Notes

- MBOs account for the majority of deals.

- In value terms, however, the picture is very different. Since 2000, MBIs have accounted for well over half of total deal value indicating a significantly higher average deal size.

Chart 1.3: MBOs and MBIs as a percentage of UK takeover activity

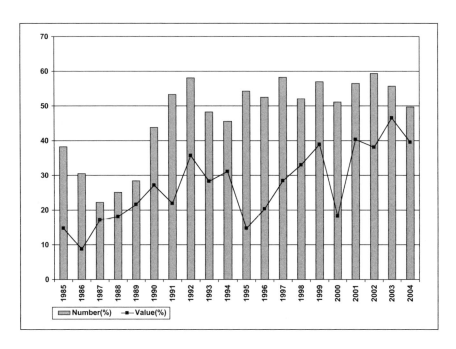

Source: CMBOR/Barclays Private Equity/Deloitte

Notes

• MBOs/MBIs dominate the number of M&A transactions in the UK, and peaked in 2002.

• The proportion of value they account for has declined recently, reflecting a significant increase in other corporate activity in 2004.

Chart 1.4: Average value of buy-outs/buy-ins (£m), 1995-2004

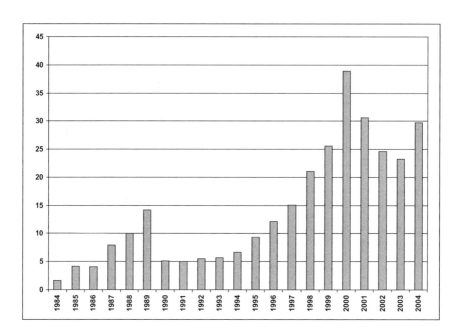

Source: CMBOR/Barclays Private Equity/Deloitte

Notes

- After declining from the peak in 2000, average deal value increased to £30m in 2004, boosted by a number of large transactions.

- Nine deals in 2004 have exceeded the £500m threshold: The AA Group £1,750m, Saga Group £1,350m, and Chelsfield £896m being the largest.

Chart 1.5: Trends of above £100m buy-outs/buy-ins, 1985-2004

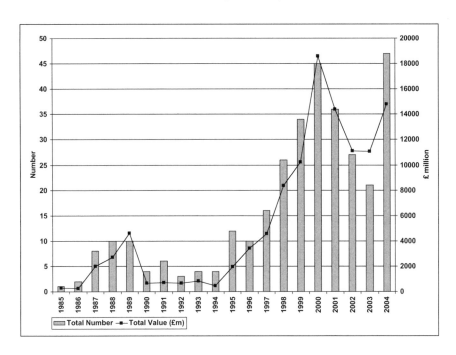

Source: CMBOR/Barclays Private Equity/Deloitte

Notes

- The trend towards larger deals is very apparent.

UK management buy-outs/buy-ins

The table below shows the significant growth in the number of transactions and the value they represent, since 1979.

Table 1.2: UK management buy-outs/buy-ins

	No.	Buy-out Val. (£m)	Avg. (£m)	Buy-in No.	Val. (£m)	Avg. (£m)	Total No.	Val. (£m)	Avg. (£m)
1979	19	22.4	1.2	1	1.5	1.5	20	23.9	1.2
1980	36	34.2	1.0	0	0.0	0.0	36	34.2	1.0
1981	146	241.0	1.7	6	26.2	4.4	152	267.2	1.8
1982	238	352.2	1.5	9	316.9	35.2	247	669.1	2.7
1983	242	391.2	1.6	10	10.6	1.1	252	401.8	1.6
1984	245	414.2	1.7	6	5.1	0.9	251	419.3	1.7
1985	263	1173.1	4.5	30	54.4	1.8	293	1227.5	4.2
1986	316	1162.9	3.7	53	316.9	6.0	369	1479.8	4.0
1987	343	3130.2	9.1	92	307.6	3.3	435	3437.8	7.9
1988	387	3806.1	9.8	114	1213.8	10.6	501	5019.9	10.0
1989	382	3895.1	10.2	148	3612.3	24.4	530	7507.4	14.2
1990	494	2452.7	5.0	112	645.0	5.8	606	3097.7	5.1
1991	456	2182.2	4.8	124	731.9	5.9	580	2914.1	5.0
1992	461	2574.2	5.6	137	731.5	5.3	598	3305.7	5.5
1993	392	2076.2	5.3	99	700.5	7.1	491	2776.7	5.7
1994	415	2618.0	6.3	150	1128.5	7.5	565	3746.5	6.6
1995	383	2983.4	7.8	215	2638.6	12.3	598	5622.0	9.4
1996	439	3704.1	8.4	207	4157.3	20.1	646	7861.4	12.2
1997	460	4569.3	9.9	247	6103.1	24.7	707	10672.4	15.1
1998	472	4817.2	10.2	216	9693.1	44.9	688	14510.3	21.1
1999	465	8066.4	17.3	188	8618.9	45.8	653	16685.3	25.6
2000	444	9534.7	21.5	170	14377.8	84.6	614	23912.5	38.9
2001	455	8812.8	19.4	183	10731.1	58.6	638	19543.9	30.6
2002	475	4483.3	9.4	153	10999.6	71.9	628	15482.9	24.7
2003	522	4124.7	7.9	178	12142.3	68.2	700	16267.0	23.2
2004	474	8816.8	18.6	213	11609.6	54.5	687	20426.4	29.7

Source: CMBOR/Barclays Private Equity/Deloitte

Table 1.3: MBOs above £100m in 2004

Buy-out name	Value (£m)	Buy-out source	Month
Saga Group	1350	Secondary Buy-out	Oct.
Chelsfield (Duelguide)	896	Public-Private	Apr.
New Look (Trinitybrook)	699	Public-Private	Mar.
DFS Furniture Company	507	Public-Private	Oct.
Swift Advances	314	Founder	May
Regent Medical	173	SSL International	Jun.
Southern Cross Healthcare	162	Secondary Buy-out	Sep.
Jarvis Hotels (Kayterm)	159	Public-Private	Jan.
Survitec Group/SGL Holdings	146	Secondary Buy-out	Aug.
Amalgamated Metal Corp	139	TUI AG (Germany)	Jan.
Morris Homes/Morris Group	127	Secondary Buy-out	Mar.
Swarfega/Deb Group/Dualwise	120	Secondary Buy-out	Mar.
Hillarys Blinds/Hillarys Group	115	Secondary Buy-out	Aug.
Delaware International	112	Lincoln National Corp	May
Hobbs	111	Secondary Buy-out	Nov.
Cabot Financial	107	Secondary Buy-out	Jan.
Burndene Investments	102	Public-Private	Mar.
Red Funnel Group	102	Secondary Buy-out	May
Iris Software	102	Secondary Buy-out	Jul.

Source: CMBOR/Barclays Private Equity/Deloitte

Table 1.4: MBIs (including IBOs) above £100m in 2004

Buy-out name	Value (£m)	Buy-out source	Month
The Automobile Association (AA)	1750	Centrica plc	Oct.
Four Seasons Healthcare	775	Secondary Buy-out	Aug.
Baxi Group	663	Secondary Buy-out	Feb.
Weetabix (Latimer)	642	Public-Private	Jan.
Autobar	535	Kuwait Investment Office	Jul.
Odeon	380	Entertainment Group & Rotch	Aug.
International Management Group (IMG)	379	Shareholders	Nov.
Dunlop Standard Engine Repair & Overhaul Business	376	Partial secondary buy-out – 98345	Sep.
IMO Carwash	350	Secondary Buy-out	Jan.
Safety-Kleen	274	Secondary Buy-out	Aug.
Maplin Electronics	244	Secondary Buy-out	Aug.
Alcontrol	240	Secondary Buy-out	Nov.
Condor Ferries	240	Secondary Buy-out	Sep.
Pets at Home	230	Founder: Mr Anthony Preston	Jul.
Shanks (UK)/Shanks & McEwan and Caird Environmental	228	Shanks Group plc	May
Paramount Hotels/ Dawnay Shore Hotels	215	Secondary Buy-out	Jul.
Global Solutions/GSL	208	Group4Falck (Denmark)	Jun.
Ask Central/Riposte	207	Public-Private	May
United Cinemas International	182	Univeral Studios/ Viacom international	Sep.
Park Resorts	165	Secondary Buy-out	Dec.
Manor Kingdom	150 (Est)	Private: Keith punter	Nov.
HSS Service Group	145	Davis Service Group	Jan.
Ethel Austin	122	Secondary Buy-out	Jun.
Cine UK/Cineworld UK	120	Shareholders	Oct.
GB Holiday Parks	105	Secondary Buy-out	Nov.
Hays Logistics	102	Hays PLC	Feb.
Jimmy Choo	101	Secondary Buy-out	Nov.
Buy as You View	n.d.	Founder: Richard Jones	Jul.

Source: CMBOR/Barclays Private Equity/Deloitte

The Deal Funnel

Figure 1.2: The Deal Funnel

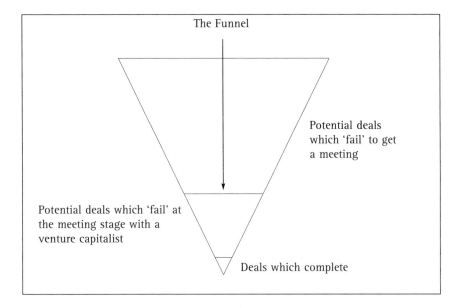

The figures in the previous table are based on deals which actually completed. This takes no account of the considerably larger number of potential deals which fail to make it for several reasons.

There aren't any hard and fast figures on the size of the funnel, but, talking to several venture capitalists on the subject, the following is a rule of thumb:

- For every 100 potential deals seen on paper, roughly 10 result in a meeting for the venture capitalist.
- For every 10 teams met, on average 1 may progress to completion.

Venture capitalists are acutely aware of The Funnel and are constantly hunting around for potential deals. They have the challenge of deciding how best to allocate their time between prospecting for deals and consummating them.

There is a very active network of venture capitalists and advisors who are constantly browsing the shelves of companies for sale.

Chapter 2

Finding a Deal

This chapter deals with how management teams can set about finding potential MBOs/MBIs.

How opportunities arise

The opportunity for an MBO/MBI may arise in a number of ways.

- A group may decide to sell a business because it has become non-core.

- A company may find itself in difficulties and need to sell all or part of the business.

- The owner of a private company wishes to retire.

- A receiver or administrator may sell a business as a going concern.

- A board may elect to leave the public arena (P2P).

- Changes in a management team, or a venture capitalist's desire to exit, may generate a secondary MBO/MBI.

Sources of MBOs/MBIs

Chart 2.1: Sources of management buy-outs/buy-ins (%) 2000-2004

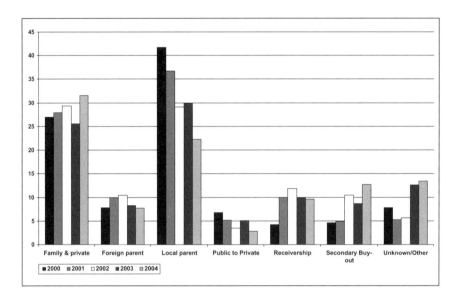

Source: CMBOR/Barclays Private Equity/Deloitte

Notes

- Sale by family controlled or private companies have spawned the most MBOs/MBIs recently.

- Plcs disgorging unwanted divisions is the second most prolific source.

- Secondary MBOs/MBIs are increasing.

Table 2.1: Sources of all UK management buy-outs/buy-ins (%)

Source Group	1995	1996	1997	1998	1999	2000	2001	2002	2003	2004
Family and private	39.0	36.9	40.2	40.7	36.1	27.1	28.0	29.4	25.4	30.9
Foreign parent	9.5	6.7	7.2	7.0	4.6	7.8	10.1	10.4	8.3	7.9
Local parent	32.6	34.0	31.0	31.5	36.0	41.6	36.5	28.8	30.0	21.9
Privatisation	2.5	5.1	2.7	0.6	0.0	0.0	0.2	0.0	0.4	0.2
Public buy-in	1.2	0.6	0.8	0.9	0.3	0.8	0.3	0.2	0.3	0.6
Public to private	0.5	0.6	1.0	3.8	7.0	6.9	5.2	3.5	5.2	3.5
Receivership	4.5	4.2	3.3	2.9	2.8	4.2	10.1	11.8	9.9	10.6
Secondary buy-out	4.8	6.2	5.9	6.1	5.8	4.6	4.9	10.4	8.6	13.4
Unknown	5.4	5.7	7.9	6.5	7.4	7.0	4.9	5.6	11.8	10.9

Source: CMBOR/Barclays Private Equity/Deloitte

Private companies

It is usually, but not always, easier to buy a private company, as they are not ensnared by the protocols and regulations (e.g. offer periods) of a public company.

There are over 1.8 private companies in the UK – over **700 times** as many as there are listed ones on the London Stock Exchange.

As explained earlier, the main source of MBOs/MBIs is private owners, who decide to sell for a variety of reasons.

Invariably the most straight forward deal is when a management team is able to buy their company as a going concern from the owner, who in many cases may have been their day-to-day boss. If you are working in such a company it is always worth exploring the potential of buying the business. With colleagues you will have a very good understanding of the owner's agenda, and also, of course, of the business potential and what makes it tick.

As covered in chapter 9, Maybridge, Webb's Country Foods and Ashford Colour Press were all bought from private companies.

No two owners are the same of course, but their options for realising capital from their business are limited to a few tried and tested routes. Selling to their management team has a number of practical advantages:

- a proven business model exists which provides new funders with comfort;

- less disruption to the business;

- tax planning for the vendor; and

- a lower risk transaction.

MBI teams hunting a deal also know this to be the most fertile territory and scan extensively for opportunities through their networks.

BIMBOs are common in the private company arena, and are frequently the case when a management team is missing an important member (e.g. a finance director). If you have the opportunity to buy the company in which you are presently working, it is relatively easy to find and attract a new team member – especially with the promise of sweet equity. The advisory community is always happy to introduce candidates to you – especially if this increases the probability of a deal being done. Maybridge was a BIMBO and its story is covered in a later chapter.

Public companies

As with all potential deals, the incumbent management team are in the ringside seats if a sale is in prospect. There has been a marked increase in the number of P2P deals completed in recent years as plcs have sought to refocus their businesses, or shareholders have agitated

There are presently 2430 companies listed on the London Stock Exchange: approximately 1,400 on the Main Market and 1,000 on AIM.

for an exit, when no trade buyer is interested. The next chapter covers some of the issues you will come across in attempting to do a deal in this sector.

Chapter 9 describes MBOs at Taunton Cider, Dennis-Eagle and Cloverleaf Group, all of which were bought from public companies.

Table 2.2: Public to private buy-outs/buy-ins 1985-2004

Year	Number	Number (% of all deals)	Value (£m)	Value (% of all deals)
1985	1	0.3	60	4.9
1986	2	0.5	34	2.3
1987	4	0.9	478	13.9
1988	8	1.6	478	9.5
1989	13	2.5	3536	47.1
1990	10	1.7	348	11.2
1991	6	1.0	57	2.0
1992	3	0.5	36	1.1
1993	1	0.2	4	0.1
1994	3	0.5	187	5.0
1995	3	0.5	48	0.9
1996	4	0.6	32	0.4
1997	7	1.0	390	3.7
1998	26	3.8	2524	17.4
1999	46	7.0	4620	27.7
2000	42	6.8	9363	39.2
2001	33	5.2	4903	25.1
2002	22	3.5	2691	17.4
2003	36	5.2	3838	23.6
2004	19	3.0	3498	17.4

Source: CMBOR/Barclays Private Equity/Deloitte

Research

"Time spent on reconnaissance is rarely wasted in the field" is an old military saying, but it applies equally to commercial life.

Before the advent of the internet, research was difficult and was dominated by professional research companies. Nowadays it is possible for anyone who knows how to use a computer to build a detailed insight into any commercial organisation quickly and cost effectively.

Personal networks

These are still as effective as ever at providing information and identifying opportunities. A combination of phone calls and meetings with employees, advisors, suppliers and customers provide a valuable insight.

Trade associations, publications and exhibitions

These are another invaluable source. A combination of desk research and attending industry events can be very informative. Invariably there will be a number of industry-specific websites available.

Financial information

There are many sources which cover public and private companies:

- **Financial websites:** for example Motley Fool, FT and MoneyAM.

- **companies' own websites**

- **Companies House:** this provides access to a company's financial history as well as information on directors, shareholders and financial performance; and

- **search engines:** Google, Yahoo and others are extremely effective as research tools. Perhaps too much so – sometimes it is like trying to fill a cup from the Niagara Falls!

Marketing sources

In certain companies advertising and promotions are vital ingredients to the business, and there are many sources of information available which can build a picture.

A company's record in advertising (level of expenditure and consistency of creative executions) is always revealing. Good brands tend to be consistently supported with strong creative executions and campaigns. Weaker, struggling brands leave tell-tale signs of erratic investment with meandering creative executions.

The integration – or lack of it – of advertising and promotional campaigns is also revealing. There should be a strong motivating message to the consumer which is evident across the marketing mix. Struggling brands will project a more confused picture.

Field visits

Trade distribution, display, appearance, promotion and pricing build a revealing picture of target and competitive brands quite quickly.

Marketing phase

Armed with information on a company's history, shareholders, structure, senior management, strategy, customers, clients, advisors, competitors and its current trading, you are in a good position to approach parties with a view to seeing whether or not a business might be for sale.

The Gatekeepers

The following are all excellent sources if you are trying to determine whether a company may be for sale:

- chairman or CEO;
- directors and senior managers;
- shareholders;
- key customers;
- suppliers;
- accountants;
- lawyers;
- banks;
- trade commentators;
- ex-employees;
- marketing agencies; and
- competitors.

Individual approach

There are legion examples of MBOs/MBIs which have been achieved by one driven person. In the case of finding MBIs there are many individuals who, perhaps having completed one deal successfully, are keen to 'twist' and do another. As covered under 'Research' above, you can see that, even alone, one person can carry out a substantial amount of preparatory work on a target company.

Team approach

Management teams run businesses, and venture capitalists prefer to back teams rather than individuals. MBI teams, especially, hunt as duos or in small packs.

Despite Lord Hanson's cynical view that "synergies are like yetis, everyone talks about them but no one has ever seen one", teams in MBOs/MBIs need to be genuinely synergistic.

Stalking a target

Armed with the information covered above, there are a number of ways of approaching a target. It is important to be credible and not perceived, either by potential backers or vendors, as a time waster.

Recommended strategy

John Webster, founder of The Chief Executives Office, has an excellent track record in advising individuals and teams on how best to pursue an MBO/MBI.

He outlines the following approach as one most likely to yield success.

1. Meet with a venture capitalist to discuss a target you have researched and have reason to believe may be available.

2. Venture capitalists allocate their time preciously. They are far more likely to meet you to discuss a specific opportunity.

3. Your aim is to secure provisional agreement to a funding package between upper and lower thresholds.

4. Armed with a letter from a venture capitalist, which confirms you have conditional financial backing, you are in a position to seek a meaningful meeting with the chairman/CEO/shareholders of your target company.

Too many managers, seeking an MBI in particular, fail to do this. Meetings with venture capitalists or potential vendors need to have a purpose. The approach outlined above provides a focal point and a reason to meet.

Note: A later chapter discusses a model I have developed which, by looking at a number of criteria and weighting them, produces a score for the analysed company. This is an exercise well worth carrying out on any target company; you can see how it compares to the seven 'Real Deals' covered in this book. It will also put the target company's relative strengths and weaknesses into perspective.

Chapter 3

Getting in Shape for the Deal

This chapter focuses on the ingredients considered vital if you are to maximise your chances of success.

The Eight Ps

Graham Spooner, a very experienced and widely respected venture capitalist, lists his 'Eight Ps' as the necessary ingredients to make an MBO/MBI successful:

1. **Potential in the quality of the business** – growth prospects.

2. **Product and process** – what you do and how you do it.

3. **People** – quality of the management team to deliver.

4. **Personal commitment and personal chemistry** to each other – the company and the venture capitalist.

5. **Projected positive cashflow** – from sustainable profits.

6. **Defensible position** in the market place – is it sustainable.

7. **Policing** – effective control and corporate governance.

8. **Prospects for an exit** – trade or private equity sale, secondary buy-out or buy-in, or flotation.

Source: Venture Capital and Private Equity – A Practitioner's Manual

I wholeheartedly endorse this list.

A strong and united management team

Sir Robert Smith, when at Morgan Grenfell Development Capital, famously said:

> *"I back three things in an MBO: management, management and management."*

Enough said!

Another way of putting this is that poor management teams can wreck a good business, while a strong team have a chance of turning around a weak and failing company.

Vendor vacuum

Many vendors, especially of private companies, are very strong and dominant characters. These are the revered owner-drivers. Whilst some have common failings (appointing Yes-Men as subordinates being a classic), I'd suggest most are central as the driving force within the business. After they leave their company there can be a dangerous vacuum left.

This problem can be exacerbated if a member of the old team is promoted to become the new managing director – often more in hope than realistic expectation that they will grow into the role. Some

> Webb's Country Foods Ltd suffered from such a vacuum when a very dominant owner driver exited successfully. The managing director anointed by him to lead the MBO simply couldn't generate the same level of drive.

do, but many don't – with pretty disastrous consequences for the business.

Ideally this would be identified, and addressed, pre-completion, but often, in a desire to get the deal done, it is swept under the boardroom carpet to be addressed later. 'Address it later' is far easier said than done.

Plug the gaps in your management team

The vendor vacuum may not be the only gap in the management team. For instance, if the company being bought is being separated from a large corporate group, there may be no treasury function in place. Given the paramount importance of cash in any MBO/MBI, this is an essential gap to plug.

This was the case at Ashford Colour Press, where the MBO team didn't have a finance boss within it. A candidate was quickly found and appointed, but unfortunately he didn't come up to scratch and had to be replaced within four months.

A more sensitive issue is whether all the members of your present team are actually capable enough. This is potentially a very difficult and divisive area. If there are significant concerns, they are best addressed and resolved before you proceed. This is for three main reasons:

1.   Backers will find them out anyway and confront you with the problem - probably not at a time of your choosing.

2.   You will increase the chances of failure markedly if you proceed with a weakened team in what is, even with a strong team, a high-risk venture.

3.   Making management changes after completion is often difficult and more expensive. It might also prove to be too late.

It may appear brutal, but having seen executive directors changed in different companies, both before and after completion, I am in no doubt whatsoever as to the right course of action. This proved to be the case at Taunton Cider's MBO, where the finance director was not invited into the deal as a principal. This was seen as a ruthless move at the time, but it proved to be the right decision.

Feet to the fire

As management you will be expected to personally invest in the deal. These days investors like to see a significant, though not potentially ruinous, investment by the principals. It aligns management's interests with theirs, and focuses the top team on the exit before the deal is completed.

Ensure you are in a position to do so. There are many ways in which funds for your investment can be generated. Here are just a few:

• In the case of an MBO, the vendor might pay the management team a success fee, especially if you had to win an auction to buy your company.

• The bank(s) providing the senior debt can be approached for a soft loan.

• The principals' remuneration can be increased to service any personal debt which is necessary.

• You could increase your mortgage.

Sharing out the sweet equity amongst the management team

There are a number of key issues to consider here.

Share amongst the principals

Usually equity would be shared broadly in relation to remuneration, since the latter should be a reliable indicator of the relative contribution of managers to the corporate effort.

Involvement of other senior managers considered important to the business

This is difficult because there is rarely enough equity to be given to all senior and middle managers. To invite only some to invest can be very divisive; managers have an uncanny knack of discovering what their peers earn!

Employees

At Taunton Cider we gave all employees the opportunity to qualify for shares in two ways. There was a free share issue to all full-time employees, which was augmented by a formal Sharesave scheme. Red tape and administration costs tend to render these measures prohibitively expensive in small companies. However, if it can be done, it can have a galvanising effect on the whole company.

Retention for potential additions to the management team in the future

This is important to bear in mind as the promise of sweet equity when trying to hire senior people is a very attractive carrot.

There can be some snags involving tax beyond completion. Many companies and their advisors have had some interesting discussions with the *Share Valuation* division of the Inland Revenue. The Inland Revenue may seek to argue after completion that the value of the shares has increased and therefore a new director, who pays the same amount as the original directors, could be said to have received a benefit-in-kind.

There are other ways of using equity-based incentives to attract and incentivise new managers. Unfortunately, the government has made Inland Revenue approved schemes too complex, too costly or too miserly to work. Therefore it's usually better to accept that tax will be paid, and to put something in place which is effective regardless.

Phantom options are a very simple and effective way of achieving this. In short, the company offers to pay an individual, based on certain conditions (e.g. change of control of the company), a cash bonus. The bonus will be calculated with reference to a number of phantom shares multiplied by the difference between the starting price of the shares and the current price when the specified conditions are met.

Chapter 4

Doing the Deal –
a White-Knuckle Ride

You should assume that it will take between six and nine months to complete your chosen deal. In the heady days of the dot com boom, funds could be raised by management teams – unencumbered by old-economy thinking – with a dozen PowerPoint slides in a very short time. Although those times have passed, there are a number of prescribed steps which must be taken and the process needs to be well managed.

Mentally and physically it is a very demanding process. There are many difficult and time-consuming tasks to be completed, which require substantial input from the management team. In addition, it will be an emotional roller coaster as the vision of completion, and you now owning your beloved company, will lurch around like a drunk after closing time.

Business plan and strategy

Your business plan:

> *"Never mind the quality, feel the length."*

A frequent complaint from those who study business plans for a living is how poor many of them are. Too many make a virtue out of length instead of clarity.

Good business plans

Good business plans contain the following:

- An **executive summary** covering succinctly and in plain English: strategy; key points about the business and management; and the situation with the vendor.
- A concise **history of the business.**
- **Strategy**: company vision and long-term objectives/milestones.
- **Market statistics**, history and trends.
- **Competitors, market share, mergers and acquisitions.**
- **Customers and debtors profile.**
- **Operations**, production and supply chain and creditors' profile.
- **Management profile**, company organisation and culture.

- **Summary of financial results** over the last two years, budget and latest forecast for the current year and projections for the next three years (profit and loss account, cashflow and balance sheet).

- Summary of **exit options**.

The projections should be positive, credible and specific. Where these show rapid growth or a change in the nature of operations, the background and reasoning will need to be clearly detailed.

An indication of likely acquisition cost should be included if known, together with any further funding requirements. It is generally not appropriate to outline funding structure.

Your business strategy

There are many books and essays devoted to this subject (please refer to the *Recommended reading* at the back of the book). I don't intend to cover this crucial topic here other than to say, as part of the business plan, it needs to be succinctly and convincingly explained. The points below are, nonetheless, a guide.

- "If it can't be written on one side of A4 it can't be understood" – Warren Buffett is alleged to have said.

- "A company's strategy is a compass not a route map", Alan Leighton.

- The description of strategy needs to pass what Americans call the *elevator test*. In other words, if you can't explain it in twenty seconds it's too complicated.

- Brevity and clarity are the guiding principles.

- As Mark Twain said: "a good impromptu speech takes at least three weeks to prepare." And so it is with strategy.

Advisors: assembling your team

Almost all the parties I have spoken to in the process of writing this book would advise that your first step is to appoint your own corporate advisors. This is most likely to be an accountancy firm who have the skills in-house, or a corporate advisory boutique. There are many to choose from. Ask your personal network and aim to get an advocated introduction.

The Ringmasters: the corporate advisers

"Good advisers are worth the money. For most people this is a once in a lifetime deal and you simply cannot afford to mess it up."

Ron Gardner, One-London Ltd

Two things are paramount in the management team's choice of corporate advisors:

1. **Personal chemistry**

   It is crucial that you can gel with the main players. Mutual respect and trust will be essential. Ensure they pass the *pint test* (i.e. would you enjoy going out to the pub with them?).

2. **The advisors' track record**

   Interrogate this. Most advisors will need little encouragement to share with you their previous experience and successes. In the case of smaller practices this is particularly important. You will be relying on them not only to guide you through the deal, but also to be able to attract and assemble a corporate team capable of achieving the deal in prospect.

There are sector specialists which might be appropriate if the target business lies in a particular niche.

Don't be afraid to ask for references. As a management team, and as individuals, you will be referenced every which way possible. Do it in reverse – find out what they are really like.

The venture capitalist

"You are not just acquiring money, but also the involvement and expertise of the venture capital firm."

Sarah Eaton, British Venture Capital Association

In February 2003, private equity houses Candover and Cinven bought the bingo clubs and casinos operator Gala Clubs for £1.24bn from its existing backers, PPM Ventures and CSFB. For Gala Chief Executive John Kelly, the transaction was the third, and by far the biggest, private equity deal of his tenure at the company.

John Kelly's advice to any entrepreneur looking to follow the private equity route is to check out the venture capitalists as closely as possible. According to him:

"You should do an extraordinary amount of due diligence on your VC. Always stay in charge as much as you can, and don't let anyone take the ball off your toe. But most of all, be absolutely up-front with your VCs before the deal and make sure you get the same openness from them."

John Kelly's advice is sound. In fact, I would argue that the venture capitalist is your most important partner in any MBO/MBI. Why? Because you have more in common with them than any other party on your deal. In short, you are going to swim or sink together.

The bank – financing the debt

The bank, or banks, on the deal is another very important partnership to be developed and nurtured, and will most probably be introduced by your corporate advisors. Venture capitalists will also have contacts with whom they have forged good working relationships.

If you have a harmonious relationship with your present clearing bank it makes sense to minimise disruption to on-going business and give them the opportunity of pitching for the business. All the major UK banks have specialist corporate teams who are always keen and hungry to secure quality deals.

Once again, the quality of the personal relationships is very important. The frequency with which you will meet the bank after completion will probably be in inverse proportion to your performance. If you perform above plan, and make your interest and capital repayments on time and in full, you will only see them occasionally.

If, on the other hand, you get into a work-out situation (covered in a later chapter), you will be seeing a lot of the bank(s), and the quality of the personal relationships developed in the past will come into play.

The lawyers

"And God said: Let there be Satan, so people don't blame everything on me. And let there be lawyers, so people don't blame everything on Satan."

George Burns.

Your legal team also has a vital role to play. As with other advisors you should be demanding in your choice. Obviously their principal role is to produce the necessary documentation; however, high quality and experienced lawyers can add value in a number of ways:

- Sage advice on the negotiations with the venture capitalists on equity split between the institution and management.

- Personal protection on warranties and indemnities.

- Guidance on the negotiations with the bank(s) on facilities.

- Overview on the process and guidance on when to say 'no'.

- Tactics with the vendors.

They are also the *only advisors* who are undoubtedly on your side throughout the entire process. All other parties will, necessarily, be on the opposite side of the table at some stage in the process. The corporate advisors will argue this point, but in my experience there are times when they have to take a broader view to get the deal done, which is after all supposedly in everyone's best interests, and sometimes they will pressurise the management team into making concessions.

Auction-busting!

Most vendors will be advised to run an auction to create competition for their company and, in doing so, maximise the price achieved. In a public company, it is a given that, in all but the most exceptional circumstances, an auction must be run to prove that shareholders' returns have been maximised.

However, occasionally management teams can appeal to a vendor's better nature and convince him that an auction is unnecessary. It might be that the loyalty card, in the case of an MBO, or fears of major disruption to the business will bust an auction.

This obviously requires a considerable act of faith on both sides, as valuation will be determined by analysts and accountants rather than the market. One major advantage to both sides in this situation though is time saved – which can often translate into lower professional fees.

The Ashford Colour Press MBO was a good example of an uncontested deal. It was conducted well and both sides were happy with the end result.

Anti-embarrassment clauses can be a means of overcoming a logjam on pricing negotiations. This can provide comfort to a vendor that he is not being shafted on price. It works by prescribing an additional sum (or sums) which becomes payable to the vendor in the event the new owners of his business sell it on, within a set time period, at a price considerably greater than they paid for it.

Highlights and stages of the six to nine month MBO/MBI process

Table 4.1: Stages in the MBO/MBI process

Stage	Management	Advisors	Documents	Watch out for….
First steps	Assembling the team. Are we 'up for it'? Initial business Plan. Tentative chats with owner(s).	Meet and 'select' your corporate advisors.	Provisional business plan.	Is the team strong enough? Personal chemistries with advisors.
'Bonding'	Refine and complete business plan. Discuss and agree terms with advisors.	Appoint your corporate team i.e. advisors & lawyers. Meet potential VCs and bankers. Each will be weighing up management and the company.	Final business plan.	Abort fees-who pays? You need a cost-indemnity. The 'Terms-sheet' – managements' share of the equity cake.
First approach	Supplying more information.	Engage vendor. Establish likely process. Timing and price expectations.	Agree final terms with the VC.	Vendor's intentions. Auction process unless you can 'bust-it'?
They're off!!!	Identifying additional Board members e.g. NXD's. Presentations and meetings with backers. Discussions with major suppliers and customers.	Submit Round 1 bid with conditions in offer letter. Contact with vendors advisors.	Heads of terms between vendor and management.	Winner of round 1 might not get an exclusive period in which to complete the deal. There could be round 2 or even 3.
End of auction	Vendor grants you an exclusive period in which to complete.	Due diligence process. Final terms agreed. Final binding offer.	Due diligence report.	VCs reducing the price they are prepared to pay. Vendor changing his mind.
Pre-completion	Final negotiations with backers. Final negotiations with major suppliers and/ or customers.	Final negotiations. Drafting and agreement of all documentation.	Memorandum and articles. Investment agreement. Banking documentation. trading agreements.	Personal warranties and restrictive covenants. Under-performance clauses/swamping rights. Completion always at 3am!
Post-completion	Briefings with employees, client/ customers/creditors. First board meeting. Investor relations.	Syndication of equity/debt. Monitoring.	Final company arrangements.	Even more presentations to syndicate the funding.

Elephant traps to avoid

"Only a fool learns from his own mistakes – a wise man learns from the mistakes of others"

Otto von Bismarck.

There are many to watch out for! It is the responsibility of your corporate advisors to point most of them out and to suggest how best to navigate around them. The proposed non-executive directors can also add value as they bring their experience to bear.

The price you pay?

There are entire books dedicated to the controversial topic of: 'How much is a company worth?' As one maxim goes: a company is worth what someone is willing to pay for it. But this, of course, may not equate to what a vendor is willing to sell it for. In the private company sector, owner drivers can have fairly inflexible views on what they are prepared to let it go for. After all, they may have spent the best part of a working lifetime building their business; understandably their view of value can be a country mile removed from an acquirer's bid price (bearing in mind the models used by venture capitalists will usually set a limit on the price which can be paid).

Similarly, from the purchaser's side, there is always a danger that the infamous models used by the venture capitalists will control pricing to such a degree that the deal may be lost.

> A venture capitalist's model on Merrydown couldn't offer above 45p a few years ago, despite aggressive growth projections. The business was sold earlier this year for £1.70 a share.

Therefore, management teams should try and establish as early in the process as they can what the vendors range of expectations are.

Realistic expectations of value are extremely important to both sides in an MBO/MBI transaction.

> As Adam Attwood of ISIS Private Equity told me, "Over-paying for any business, supported by a leveraged structure, is the single biggest reason why MBOs and MBIs fail".

It is difficult enough for a leveraged company to withstand a financial shock from an unplanned event, for example a recall from trade of a brand or loss of a contract. If the business is also labouring under a debt structure, already obese from paying a high price, the combination is usually fatal.

Costs: levels

 The advisory market is very competitive. Have the confidence to negotiate with your advisors over fees; never accept their opening offer! If you have appointed your non-executive directors, then use their experience to reduce costs. An experienced non-executive should more than pay for his fees here.

 Consider fixed fees which are becoming increasingly common, especially with lawyers and accountants. Paying by the meter, rather than a fixed rate for the journey, can be very expensive.

Costs: indemnity

It is crucial that you agree who is going to pay costs if the deal fails to complete.

It is said some teams have been horribly caught out and ended up paying large fees out of their own pockets. Failing to complete a deal is demotivating enough – you can do without the additional pain of significant fees to pay.

There are two main ways to protect your position:

1. Get an **indemnity from the vendor**. In other words, if he pulls out of your deal for any reason then he will pay all of the management's costs up to that point.

 2. Agree **'no success, no fee' deals** with your team of advisors. This, however, can have the understandable drawback of putting some advisors off your deal. You should bear in mind that advisors only complete a fraction of all the deals they consider, therefore, if their remuneration is wholly dependent upon completing a deal, they are very choosy about which deals they will run with.

The vendor changes his mind

This can happen equally in the public and private company sectors – and for reasons far beyond your control. Circumstances change and the business is no longer for sale. Few things can be as disheartening as working extremely hard for six months, only to have the rug pulled from beneath you at the eleventh hour.

The dysfunctional team

The pressures of getting a deal done will test any management team to its limit. Even teams which are normally stable, mutually supportive and content find the process very challenging. If the team is riven with ancient rivalries or major personality clashes, the process may well expose these. You need a strong team to complete a deal. An autocratic boss, with five direct reports instead of a genuine team, will have an uphill struggle.

In a later chapter the dysfunctional teams at Cloverleaf Group and Tubex are covered. In both cases, directors caused significant problems, with adverse consequences for the business.

Major suppliers and customers/clients

Depending on the business, these parties have different roles to play.

 Investors, as part of due diligence, will wish to carry out thorough referencing on the management team and business through the eyes of major customers.

In the case where a small number of customers account for a majority of sales, then *supply* or *trading agreements* may well be required to help reduce risk to acceptable levels. If the vendors are major suppliers or customers then formal agreements, or a *condition precedent*, will almost certainly be mandatory for any deal.

In the case of the Taunton Cider MBO, shareholders were also major customers. Thus long-term supply agreements with Bass and Courage became *condition precedents* in getting the deal done.

It goes without saying, therefore, that relationships with major customers, clients and suppliers need to bear close scrutiny in the due diligence process.

Who's minding the shop?

The principals in any deal will be very heavily distracted for an average period of six to nine months. Their availability to the business could fall by two or three days a week for this period; the potential pitfalls here are obvious to any manager.

While the cat's away...

MBOs/MBIs present an opportunity for competitors to exploit weaknesses in your business. Apart from the fact that you will be distracted trying to get your deal done, customers and suppliers can be unsettled by competitors drawing their attention to your present instability and imminent precarious financial structure.

Your share of the cake

As covered in the first chapter, the sweet equity is where the potential value resides if your MBO/MBI is successful. The split of this equity will be enshrined in the *investment agreement* (also known as the *subscription agreement* or *shareholders agreement*) between the venture capitalist and the management team. It will, at some stage in the process, be the subject of a robust negotiation between both parties.

> The relationship between the venture capitalists and management share of equity is also known as the *envy* or *greed ratio*.

You need to be well-advised on this negotiation for reasons which are self-evident.

Sometimes a ratchet mechanism is agreed upon to incentivise management to maximise the price achieved upon the exit. Put simply, the management's share of equity can be stepped depending on the price achieved on the sale of the business. At a sale price of, say, £20m, management may be entitled to a 20% share; with an additional 1 percentage point with every additional million pound achieved, up to a maximum of 30%. However, these can also be agreed in reverse!

Banking agreements

These can be complicated – especially to a non lawyer or banker – as they are designed to maximise the bank's security, and at the same time give the company the most headroom with its facilities, although these can be conflicting objectives! As with the investment agreement between the venture capitalist and management, the banking agreements will be the subject of quite demanding negotiations.

The banks use *covenants* to measure how well a company is performing. These are a series of backward looking financial hurdles the company must clear. Normally around half a dozen measures will be agreed, with the targets tending to become more demanding over time – especially if performance is below plan.

Some typical examples of covenants are shown below.

- **Senior interest cover**

    For example: a ratio of 3:1. The twelve month rolling PBIT should be at least 3 times greater than the twelve month rolling total of interest on senior debt, hire-purchase and lease commitments.

- **Total interest cover**

    For example: a ratio of 2.5:1. The twelve month rolling PBIT should be at least 2.5 times greater than the twelve month rolling total of interest on all debt.

- **Tangible net worth**

    For example: the total of net assets and goodwill will always exceed a given figure.

The best way of managing the covenants when running an MBO/MBI is to graph them, which shows quickly and clearly how close to the wind the company is sailing.

Personal warranties/restrictive covenants

Jeremy Gough and Mark Weston, both very experienced venture capitalists, when dealing with us on the Taunton Cider MBO memorably described our personal warranties as a truth drug.

In essence, the warranties form an undertaking by the management team that things are as they have purported them to be. In extreme cases, if a venture capitalist believes he has been deliberately misled, he can resort to these to recover loss and damages from the management team. This is fortunately a very rare event, but the management team must pay particular attention to them. Personal warranties are not to be taken lightly.

The lawyers to the management team will advise their clients carefully in respect of this. Warranties can be watered down by a process known as *disclosure*, whereby management draws the attention of investors to potential problems (for example, potential litigation).

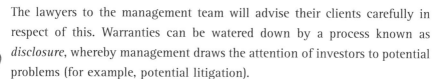

Brian Longstaff, the Taunton Cider operations director, performed admirably in this respect during the warranties and disclosures negotiations with Morgan Grenfell Development Capital. In short, we decided to disclose the board minutes from the last five years of meetings. This meant he sat up all night, fortified by a bottle or two of the law firm's claret, and walked the MGDC team through every sentence in the formidable collection of minutes! It achieved its purpose.

Restrictive covenants apply to members of the management team and to any intellectual properties in the company. As with warranties, management need to be well-advised in respect of these undertakings.

Service agreements

While most managers will have a contract of employment, or service agreement, it is often the case in an MBO/MBI that backers will wish to replace these with more comprehensive agreements.

As a management team you need to be well-advised, again by a lawyer, preferably an employment specialist, in respect of these. These will include the much-vaunted *good leaver-bad leaver* clauses, and cater for almost all possible exit scenarios of an individual. Good leavers depart with various rights intact, for example, fair value of their shares and/or options.

You will recognise a harsh agreement if it maintains that the only good leaver is a dead one!

Due diligence

This is the process carried out by potential backers of an MBO/MBI. Think of it as the equivalent of a full structural survey before buying a house. The process also provides a lifebuoy for the fund providers to the business, who are answerable to their own investors of course, and this process is mandatory. However it is far from perfect, and often management teams are at best sceptical and at worst become very unsettled and angry at the process and its cost.

Due diligence carried out by an accountancy firm, working to a very detailed questionnaire – usually prepared by the lawyers – and covers several key areas in the anatomy of a business. It is not inexpensive and, depending on how extensive a review is prescribed, costs can reach a six figure sum, even on a modest-size deal.

The main areas most likely to be covered will be:

- **Financial due diligence**
  This differs from the usual audit report in that its primary purpose is to look forward and identify potential problem areas which could adversely affect the prospects and value of the target company. The working capital review is particularly important as it needs to quantify and corroborate a prudent level of headroom in the company's facilities.

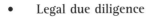

- Legal due diligence
  This focuses on predictable areas: the target company's constitution and ownership; past, current and potential litigation; contracts; intellectual property; property assets; leases and hire purchase commitments; pensions (increasingly a key area); compliance; proposed legislative changes etc.

- **Commercial due diligence**

  This can be extensive as it looks to the very core of what makes a business tick. Products, pricing, advertising and marketing, distribution, √ supply chain, production and operations, customers, clients, IT, research and development, new product development, environmental issues and managerial effectiveness can all be covered.

Like a structural survey on your house it is both a necessity and of little use if the equivalent of dry rot is subsequently discovered in the business you have bought. Warranty claims are rare after the event.

Main advantages

- A thorough MOT of the business.

- Clean bill of health on all things financial. Think of it as a super audit.

- Third party and confidential referencing on your key managers.

- Candid customer/client feedback.

- Reality check on business plan projections.

- Working capital review to ensure sufficient headroom exists within the banking facilities agreed.

- Environmental audit.

Main disadvantages

- Limited use on the effectiveness of management either as individuals or as a team.

- Given the reason most mergers and acquisitions fail is people-related, this is a potential flaw and goes some way to explaining why a significant proportion of all deals end in receivership.

- Usually the reports highlight certain weaknesses or areas for improvement. However, in the post-completion excitement these are often consigned to the FD's drawer and not acted upon. It is worth √ tasking a board member with producing a summary of the report and a plan to address the issues it has raised.

Personal references on the management team

The venture capitalists will take references on each of you in the ordinary course of business to get the deal done. They might also go to considerably more trouble to find out what you are really like!

> Jeff Bocan of Beringea Private Equity told me that – knowing a prospective managing director played amateur league soccer – he went to the trouble of tracking some of his team-mates down, to find out what Rob Hutcheson was really like! The feedback from his team-mates was excellent and the deal was duly completed.

Chapter 5

Board Structure and Behaviour

The structure, balance and performance of a board is inextricably linked to a company's performance and chances of success. A dysfunctional board will have a corrosive and negative effect on the organisation.

Good board/bad board

"Boards matter to VC firms. Why? Because Good Boards make you money while bad boards blow it away."

Patrick Dunne, 3i plc.

The best boards usually comprise of a team of highly committed folk who seem to have a passion for success in what they do. Invariably the directors have a strategy which is simple, easy to understand and passes the *elevator test* (can be clearly explained in about twenty seconds). The strategy is also being vigorously implemented and, crucially, measured so one can see milestones being passed and objectives being achieved.

Bad board behaviour displays many common traits, for example, a strategy that will never pass the elevator test – perhaps not even one which travels a hundred floors! The great 15th century Chinese General Sun Tzu said: "If you don't know where you are going any road will take you there." How true. When the board is confused on strategy, the running of the company is usually haphazard, and trying to identify progress, in any direction, is like swimming in treacle.

The table below is a quick ready-reckoner. You might spot some characteristics you recognise!

The tell-tale signs of good board/bad board

Table 5.1: Signs of good/bad boards

	Bad board	Good board
Agenda	Handed out at meeting. Long list of jumbled-up topics. Inconsistent.	Circulated with board papers. Separates information from issues and decisions. Consistent format.
Date of meeting	Ad hoc. Frequent changes and postponements.	Schedule published for a year in advance. Adhered to.
Length of meeting	< 1 hour or > 4	2 1/2 - 3 hours
Chairman	Dominates the debate. Fails to get other opinions.	Tees up issues and involves all directors. Closes down waffle. Summarises.
Board papers	Masses of data. Cluttered. Incomplete. Late.	Good information. Consistent format. Circulated 3 working days before the meeting.
Judgement	Hesitant. Poor. Lessons go unheeded.	Sound. Lessons learned.
Decision-making	Unclear. Avoided.	Positive. Clear.
Quality of debate	Limited. Spiteful.	Robust. Respectful.
Atmosphere	Cold. Defensive.	Warm. Humorous. Secure.
Behaviour	Individual. Point scoring.	Team. Collaborative. Supportive.
Minutes and follow-up	Late. Inaccurate. Long and turgid. Woolly accountability.	Draft to chairman within 2 days. Circulated within 5 days. Succinct. Clear action points.
'After-glow'	Thank-God that's over for another month. Waste of my time.	Enjoyable. Stimulating. We made progress.

Board composition

To be effective the board must be well-balanced (between executive and non-executive directors) and have all the essential skills needed to run the company. Basic, you would have thought, but boards often are populated with a cast of a dozen or so, to avoid upsetting some senior managers. Conversely, some chairmen and managing directors resist the appointment of essential players for historic reasons.

It is usually worthwhile inviting key senior managers to occasionally attend the board and for them to make a presentation on key issues.

Board calendar

Boards should be badged well in advance (e.g. the budget board). This is an essential discipline in public companies as deadlines for Interim and preliminary results concentrate the mind. In private companies, things are often less well-planned, which can naturally lead to problems (e.g. new financial year has begun before the budget has been finally agreed).

Investors in a new MBO/MBI will expect key deadlines to be met, and the senior debt providers in particular can get very twitchy and aggressive if lateness persists.

Other boards worthy of being badged are: Strategy and Long-Range Plan, Audit report, Personnel, Site and Capacity Planning, and Marketing. An example is shown over the page.

Table 5.2: Sample board calendar

Month	Focus	Comment
January	Full year 2003 review Review of professional advisors	Review of results Round-up on Brokers, bank, lawyers and auditors
February	Sales review Results + accounts for 2003	Presentation of sales strategy and plans Review of accounts, press release, dividend etc.
March	Audit Committee Risk assessment + Internal Health & Safety Review	Auditors to attend – review Control systems review of audit findings
April	Quarter 1 review Review of Q1 re-forecast	
May	Operations review Personnel review/Health & safety review	Presentation of operations strategy and plans Presentation of personnel strategy and plans + health & safety review
June	Strategy review Marketing review	Update on the company's business plan Presentation of marketing strategy and plans
July	Half Year review Review of Q2 re-forecast	Review of results
August	Audit committee	Review of interim accounts, press release, dividend etc.
September	Mergers & acquisitions + competitive review	Presentation of mergers & acquisitions strategy and review of competition
October	Quarter 3 review Review of Q3 re-forecast	
November	Outlook for 2004 & 2005 Draft budget for 2005 Remuneration committee	
December	Budget for 2005	Formal approval of budget for the new year

Board papers

These are rather like golf-swings or serves at tennis – no two are ever the same. They can vary from the excellent to the incomprehensibly awful.

The concept of a *corporate dashboard* is an excellent one, which well-managed companies often use. As the title implies, the board pack has easy to read 'dials' which convey, clearly and quickly, performance in the vital areas. No matter how complex or large a business, there will always be a dozen or so crucial measures which should be regularly monitored.

It is worth designing this pre-completion. New board members and backers have very short fuses if they are given a monthly ball of tangled wool which they need to unravel in order to understand how their new investment is performing.

The following two charts are good examples of where, in a board pack, a picture is worth a thousand words.

Chart 5.1: Example 1 of a chart in a board pack

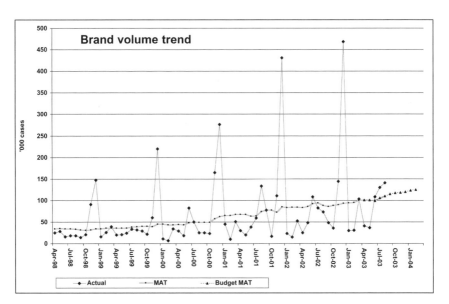

This chart uses moving annual total sales (MAT) as well as traditional monthly figures. As a result the important trend is clearly shown, as the MAT data eliminates the seasonality in the monthly numbers.

Chart 5.2: Example 2 of a chart in a board pack

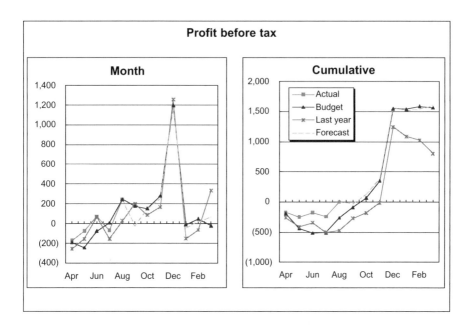

The charts above quickly inform the reader of short-term and longer-term financial performance against budget. One page like this can replace several pages of numbers.

Covenants

Consequently, the new funders of the business will set *covenants* which are a series of measures, usually applied quarterly, which measure how the business is performing against the plan. Think of them as trip-wires not to be snagged. If they are snagged or,

> Profit and cashflow is important in any business: it is critical in a business carrying substantial debt – especially one not used to doing so.

worse, completely broken, you are in the first stages of some trouble and the new backers will have been alerted as alarm bells start ringing.

I return to this unhappy scenario under the *work-out* section later in the book. Given the above, you would be forgiven for imagining that these covenants should therefore be watched pretty closely. The trouble is they are difficult to fully understand for most people, save the finance director and the more financially-aware managing director. The best solution is to graph them; in so doing they are demystified and the trend of performance against the covenants can be clearly seen. Unfortunately this seems to be the exception. More commonly a deathly hush descends on the board meeting when the question "and how are we tracking against the covenants?" is asked. In the worst cases the first thing a board may know of its transgression is when a very terse letter or phone call is received, summoning directors to the bank to explain themselves.

Communication

Technology is a great enabler and has provided the means for excellent communications amongst management teams. Listed below are some examples of how more progressive companies achieve good communications cost-effectively.

> Running a business is 20% strategy and 80% implementation. Without good communications, implementation is always going to be like dragging a wet mattress up the stairs.

- **Annual presentations** by top management on strategy (including long-term aims, major objectives and important plans) to all employees.

- **Regular presentation of financial results** to all employees.

- Use of simple, clear **PowerPoint slides**.

- Use of **PDAs** to give managers real time access to emails wherever they may be.

- A well-presented **company website**.

- **Group texting** to company mobile phones.

- Development of a **company intranet**.

- Use of company **message boards** (paper or electronic).

- **Company newsletters and in-house magazines** (paper or electronic).

> Maybridge was transformed with the arrival of a new and progressive CEO, Nick Kerton. Introduction of much of the above improved company morale hugely.
>
> Similarly the directors of the Ashford Colour Press MBO have embraced email and Blackberries. They have derived substantial benefits from better, more efficient communications.

The role of the board

From the Higgs Review 2003:

"The board is collectively responsible for promoting the success of the company by directing and supervising the company's affairs. The board's role is to provide entrepreneurial leadership of the company within a framework of prudent and effective controls which enable risk to be managed. The board should set the company's strategic aims, ensure that the necessary financial and human resources are in place for the company to meet its objectives, and review management performance. The board should set the company's values and standards and ensure that its obligations to its shareholders and others are understood and met."

In an MBO/MBI, because of the high-risk nature of the transaction, it is particularly vital that the board operates efficiently.

Chairman and non-executive directors

Chairman

Quoting from the Higgs Review 2003:

"The chairman is responsible for:

- Leadership of the board, ensuring its effectiveness on all aspects of its role and setting its agenda;

- ensuring the provision of accurate, timely and clear information to directors;

- ensuring effective communication with shareholders;

- arranging the regular evaluation of the performance of the board, its committees and individual directors; and

- facilitating the effective contribution of non-executive directors and ensuring constructive relations between executive and non-executive directors."

In an MBO/MBI the chairman, who was probably introduced to the executive directors by the venture capitalist, has additional tasks and challenges. He will normally have had experience of several leveraged deals. He needs to bring to bear the experience he has acquired to help other directors manage the pressures and challenges unique to an MBO/MBI. This is particularly the case if performance is significantly below plan and a work-out scenario begins to materialise.

The chairman should also be able to add value by bringing his M&A experience to bear on exit planning.

His personal networks might also allow the executive directors to save money and time by legitimately cutting some corners.

He will also have a key role to play in brokering agreements between management and the venture capitalist, if a refinancing is necessary, as the equity allocations may need to be reset.

Finally, he may also have to implement management change in the event of a loss of confidence in key executive directors by the backers.

The relationship between chairman and chief executive

From the Higgs Review 2003:

> "A strong relationship between the chairman and chief executive lies at the heart of an effective board. As set out in the research conducted for the Review, the relationship works best where there is a valuable mix of different skills and experiences which complement each other. The chairman should not seek executive responsibility and should let the chief executive take credit for their achievements. The chairman can be an informed, experienced and trusted partner, the source of counsel and challenge designed to support the chief executive's performance, without becoming an obstacle to questioning of the chief executive by the non-executive directors. The separation of roles can contribute to the greater achievement of the chief executive as well as being important in creating the conditions for effective performance by the non-executive directors."

In an MBO/MBI this relationship comes into very sharp relief. The CEO often relies heavily on his chairman for advice and encouragement in dealing with situations new to him and borne out of the deal itself.

Again, this is particularly the case in a scenario where the business is underperforming. The chairman must ultimately decide whether the CEO, and/or his colleagues, are capable of running the business or whether they are part of the problem. This is a truly onerous responsibility.

Non-executive directors

Higgs highlights the contribution of non-executive directors in four key areas.

1. **Strategy**: non-executive directors should constructively challenge and contribute to the development of strategy.

2. **Performance**: non-executive directors should scrutinise the performance of management in meeting agreed goals and objectives and monitor the reporting of performance.

3. **Risk**: non-executive directors should satisfy themselves that financial information is accurate and that financial controls and systems of risk management are robust and defensible.

4. **People**: non-executive directors are responsible for determining appropriate levels of remuneration of executive directors and have a prime role in appointing, and where necessary removing, senior management and in succession planning.

Whether an MBO/MBI has on its board non-executive directors in addition to the chairman is often a function of the company's size, and whether the additional overheads are thought to be both affordable and appropriate.

In my experience, with the right personal chemistry, non-executive directors add substantial value, especially when the chips are down or there are particularly difficult issues to overcome.

Too often executive directors look through the wrong end of the telescope at the cost of non-executive directors. Capable and experienced ones, of which there are many, add substantial value and, over the course of a deal, will repay their fees manyfold.

Investor relations

The investment and banking agreements will specify who is to receive what information, and by when. However, this is the bare minimum required to keep backers content. Someone once said: "When you have all the facts you have half the story." The backers expect the supporting texture and management's interpretation of results.

Also, results don't look ahead. If there are problems looming, backers expect notice to provide them with the opportunity of managing their own fund providers' expectations.

> This is a two-way street. The maxim of *no surprises* is a good one to live by. Another credo to live up to is: don't present funders with a problem – present the solution(s) at the same time.

Venture capitalists react badly if they feel either bounced into major decisions, or embarrassed by finding out about significant problems either too late or from another source, especially from the bank.

In many MBOs/MBIs the venture capitalist will appoint its own director to the board which lowers the burden of communications on the executive directors. However, in many cases this isn't possible, and instead the chairman, CEO and finance director need to agree who is going to brief the backers.

The banks will expect to receive regular information on time, and will probably, in the initial stages in particular, schedule management presentations to update them on current trading and key issues.

The amount of information requested by backers is usually inversely proportionate to performance against plan. This can become an issue as an already hard-pressed management can be soaked by requests for more analysis and information. If this is sustained for any period it is worth considering an additional pair of hands to help the finance team to produce what is required. One thing is for sure, the requests will not dry up until performance improves.

Chapter 6

Running an MBO/MBI

What's changed? Mind your four Cs

The company is now leveraged, and owes a lot of money relative to its worth to a lot of institutions. Those banks and institutions who are new creditors will be very observant, especially in the early phases, to ensure that their investment is in good hands and appears to be safe.

Management have new stakeholders whose confidence and respect needs to be retained (I say retained because the deal would not have been completed unless their confidence was already at a satisfactory level) and reinforced.

Customers and competitors

Customers and competitors will have a different perspective too. The latter usually won't be slow in promoting the view that your company is now a greater credit risk, and as such should be treated by all and sundry with the utmost caution henceforth. If you haven't checked your Moody's or Standard and Poor's credit ratings clients/customers and competitors will usually do it for you!

Colleagues and employees

Colleagues and employees are another very important group who can be overlooked in the fog of completion and its aftermath. Irrespective of the size of the organisation, they need to be engaged positively, and invariably require a level of reassurance that those young asset-strippers bedecked in pin stripes aren't about to wreck their company and livelihood.

Creditors and suppliers

Creditors and significant suppliers should be briefed on the facts and reassured as to the future. Effort made here will usually be well-rewarded – especially should the going get tough at any stage and you find yourself seeking to increase working capital with the knowledge and support of main suppliers.

Hit the ground running

Completing an MBO/MBI is a draining and tortuous process. Many compare the immediate aftermath to that feeling after exams – a sort of post-climactic emptiness.

There are other pitfalls to beware of in the after-glow of doing the deal; vendor vacuum is a prime one, already referred to earlier. Less obvious ones may come under the description, 'while the cats have been away, the mice have been at play'. The 'mice' could be: restless employees; mischievous competitors and increased raw material costs.

> The best way of combating this is to have some post-completion priorities and targets to focus the team back on the day job.

Post-completion priorities

These vary between an MBO and an MBI. Understandably the MBI team have significant additional issues to face arising from their blind date.

Table 6.1: Post-completion priorities

	MBO	MBI
Cash management	✓	✓
Outstanding post-completion issues	✓	✓
Management vacancies to be filled ASAP	✓	✓
Building relationships with employees and management		✓
Re-engaging with employees and management	✓	
Meeting customers	✓	✓
Settling down creditors and suppliers	✓	✓
Investor relations	✓	✓
Board cohesion and effectiveness	✓	✓
Discovery of, and dealing with, 'black holes'		✓
Management information		✓
Vendor vacuum		✓
Alignment of all management behind strategy		✓
Cultural problems		✓
Family and friends	✓	✓

Getting organised: the key areas to focus upon

Short-term (first twelve weeks)

1. Post-completion matters
    - Summarise all main agreements
    - Equity and debt syndication

2. Identify and plan to deal with the gap(s) left by vendor
    - Small/large company issues
    - Cash management
    - Quality and availability of management information
    - Ensure covenants understood and measured accurately
    - Plan to ration cash across the business
    - Review and confirm spending authorities

3. Strategy
    - Reality check
    - Drawn out and debilitating process pre-completion will have had an effect
    - Understanding/alignment of management and staff

4. Customers/suppliers communication

5. Stabilise staff and fill senior vacancies quickly

6. Investor relations/obligations
    - Build the relationships
    - Manage expectations
    - Don't hide bad news, but aim to present solutions together with problems
    - Clarify executive directors' authorities and board calendar

Mid-term (first twelve months)

7. Business improvement plan

   - Review objectives

   - Consider opportunities to accelerate (e.g. review margins by customer/brand and act accordingly)

   - Capitalise on due diligence findings

8. Culture change

   - Dealing with the new world

   - Review senior management carefully

   - Make necessary changes quickly

9. Delivery of plan targets

   - They should be being met by now!

Long-term (twelve months +)

10. Aims

    - To build the business within the rules (covenants) and exceed the business plan

    - To achieve value for all investors

11. Strategic review every two years

    - Consider outside facilitators

12. Capacity and capital review

    - Production and site planning

    - Review capex scale and funding

13. M&A review

    - Exit planning

    - Acquisitions

14. Corporate advisors

    - Review the team, beauty-parades

    - Exit planning and options

    - Review opportunities for growth by acquisition, hard-alliances

Unique pressures

Running any business is demanding and an MBO/MBI does bring unique pressures and problems due to the nature of the financing of the business.

> *Cash is king*: the lifeblood of MBOs/MBIs is the cash they generate. Management must identify the levers which control cash and use them to maximum effect.

Making interest and capital repayments

Repayments due on the funds borrowed, debt or equity, is a must. Failure to do so is akin to missing your mother's birthday! And no matter why you were late; you will not be able to get the toothpaste back in the tube.

Backers will react in a number of ways if you fail to keep your side of the bargain – no matter what the cause. Banks will request additional information and, ultimately, are entitled to withdraw facilities. In practice the latter, which tips the business into administration or receivership, is the saloon of last resort.

Equity providers are pragmatic about the deferment of interest due on the preferential shares, but if this proves to be long-term, and also includes default on scheduled redemption of the shares, then they too have recourse through the investment agreement to restore their margin. This may include a legitimate grab on some of management's equity or, in more extreme cases, the invocation of *swamping rights*, which effectively give them total control.

Management and employees behaviour

Even if you have incentivised several key managers, or even all employees, there will be an undercurrent of agitation which stems from the realisation that it's the principals in the MBOs/MBIs who stand to make a life-changing amount of money from the deal. Over time this will create a degree of unrest which is unavoidable.

The events at Tubex, described later, displayed this vividly.

Creditors and suppliers

They will know that since the MBO/MBI they are extending credit to a more risky enterprise. They may seek to reduce their exposure by reducing your creditor days or even by increasing their margin.

Provision of information

The rights of backers to management information will have been defined, and therefore agreed to, before completion. Investors become initially restless, and progressively bad-tempered, if it is not forthcoming in an accurate and punctual fashion. For some management teams this can be a cause of some frustration they may have, particularly in the case of businesses recently sprung from group control where they were used to being spoon-fed with information (i.e. cash managed by a group treasury function). There is no way around this – the required information simply must be produced.

> Ashford Colour Press had appointed a new finance director to the team at completion. Unfortunately it didn't work out and after three months we were still flying blind on results. We had to take very decisive action, replacing him with an experienced interim while the search for a permanent replacement got underway.

Work-life balance

The most content and efficient managers have a well-balanced life between work and home. In an MBO/MBI, where work pressures are intensified, this is particularly important.

The MBO/MBI will have had an effect on your personal life, and while partners can understand why you were distracted and working long hours leading up to completion, many find it hard to understand why this may continue to be the case after the deal is done. You need to be cognisant of this and plan your personal life accordingly.

It is accepted wisdom that the happier you are in your personal life, the more effective you will be in your professional one. Executive coaches understand the importance of this and can be a major force for good as a mentor to executive directors in an MBO/MBI.

As an executive coach to Mike Molesworth, the managing director of Dennis-Eagle, I worked hard on this with him – especially as a mini work-out phase engulfed the company after trading conditions deteriorated in their market.

At the end of the day, what's the point of making a few million if your personal life has disintegrated in the process?

Chapter 7

Success or Failure

The $64,000 question: what are your chances of success?

Venture capitalists are by nature competitive animals and thus very wary about telling you their own figures. Based on what many have said in rare moments of weakness, coupled with research at CMBOR, I believe a reasonable guesstimate to be a:

- 10% chance you will be a star;

- 15% you will succeed – but modestly;

- 50% of going sideways and wandering around in the foothills of success; and

- 25% will go bust.

The data below is compiled by CMBOR. It is a sobering thought that since 2001 most deals have exited via receivership. Every receivership is a corporate bereavement; behind these figures lays a great deal of personal angst and financial loss.

Chart 7.1: UK buy-outs/buy-ins by type of exit

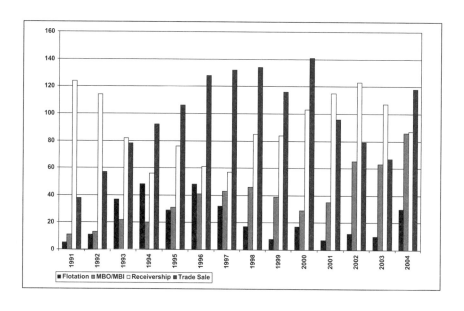

Source: CMBOR/Barclays Private Equity/Deloitte

On a more positive note, for every failure there are several which survive - although survival doesn't necessarily mean success. Secondary MBOs in particular may simply be a refinancing with a minimal uplift in value. Exits via a trade sale are commonplace; however, a proportion of these will also be at a price below, or only just above, the initial price paid some years previously.

Exit by flotation will almost certainly mean a substantial return for management and their backers. Unfortunately, for well-trailed reasons, the number of flotations in recent years has declined significantly.

You must make your budget/business plan targets

There is no shortage of reasons why any business fails to achieve its budget. In a conventionally run business it's often the case that the budget is hopelessly out of reach by the end of the first quarter and is overtaken by a re-forecast. Benjamin Disraeli is credited with saying "the only constant in life is change", and so it proves in business.

> In an MBO/MBI, below plan performance can bring very serious consequences: profit shortfall means a cash shortfall, and cash sustains companies which are heavily indebted. If cash (the lifeblood) drains away, the company will die.

Below budget performance within a division of a large group can be demanding to manage. It is usually tougher to manage in a plc where investors can be very unforgiving when their expectations are not met.

Common causes of underperformance: what are they?

I asked my Somerset County Cricket Club chairman Giles Clarke this question, after all he has had more success than just about anyone I can think of with MBOs/MBIs.

"Those that fall over are over-excited, over-geared and over-hyped."

was the answer.

The usual villains of the piece are explained below.

1. Sudden change in the market

Product failure

This is rare in most markets, but it is not unheard of. Delrosa was the staple diet of most infants in the post-war period and was still thriving until the 1980s. Then came a bolt out of the blue; the BBC's That's Life programme ran a sensationalised and misleading programme which highlighted dental decay, said to be caused by the product. The product hit the buffers very quickly.

Product availability – recall due to contamination or tampering

While unusual, this is a more common occurrence than most believe, as we only become aware of the situations which are reported by the media. Retailers routinely withdraw products and brands as a result of safety concerns which arise either by mistakes or faults in the manufacturing process, or as a result of malicious tampering by disaffected employees or criminals.

Perrier never regained its supreme position following its trade recall in 1990 as a result of the benzene contamination. Similarly, Coca-Cola's Dasani was mortally wounded in similar circumstances in 2004, when traces of bromate were found to exceed the levels permitted in the UK.

More recently, a managing director of a well-known cider and drinks manufacturer was convicted and subsequently imprisoned for an attempted contamination of Bulmer's products.

While insurance cover usually offers financial compensation to a conventionally run business, this takes time to be settled and, in particular, to quantify and agree consequential losses. For a highly geared company the time delay can be fatal, as it is not designed to withstand the shock of a sudden and significant cash shortage.

Production or supply-chain failure causes significant stock shortages

All manufacturing businesses experience problems in this area from time to time. Sometimes they may be avoidable; but often they're not. Overseas sourcing of raw materials is increasingly common for UK-based manufacturers. This significantly increases the risk of finished goods shortages. There have been many examples in recent years – the French lorry drivers' disputes still being fresh in the memory.

'Supply-chain failure' was the source of a black hole in the BIMBO at Maybridge. Antediluvian management information systems failed to measure order satisfaction appropriately, and when improvements to the system were made, and the real picture could be seen, we were horrified. (This is covered in a later chapter.)

Loss of significant distribution (e.g. a delisting by a major multiple of a grocery brand)

This is a hardy chestnut. As fewer retail chains account for an increasing share of consumer expenditure, the balance of power between suppliers and retailers has continued to tilt in favour of the latter. It brings to mind a see-saw: with an elephant on one end and a mouse on the other.

This is the stark commercial reality. Retailers increasingly have the power – whether exercised knowingly or not – to make or break many of their customers' fortunes.

This has been graphically illustrated in recent times by Marks and Spencer's trials (literally in the case of Baird Textile Holdings Ltd) and tribulations with their long-term suppliers. M&S have had to adopt a far more aggressive stance with their traditional suppliers to enable them to compete more effectively. Consequently, demands for improved trading terms and increased margins have often been achieved by squeezing their suppliers. Sometimes this can only be achieved by rationalising the number of suppliers – with dire consequences for some of them.

Cloverleaf Group was hit during the work-out phase by delistings (i.e. customers deciding to discontinue various product lines due to poor customer service and competitive actions). This made a difficult enough position even tougher.

Underestimating the impact of a new market entrant

Often, management's understandable reaction to the emergence of a new competitor is to underestimate the negative impact on their business. A good example would be the response of the established airlines to competition from the new discounters. The eclipse of the British motorcycle industry by the Japanese brands was a classic case of head-in-the-sand management. Another example was the Swiss watch industry who thought the emergence of the quartz crystal powered brigade, again from the Far East, would prove to be a passing fad!

Webb's Country Food's business plan underestimated the impact of competition from Brazil and South-East Asia on pricing in the UK poultry market. In an industry where gross margins hover around 15%, a mere five percent drop in retail pricing can be the difference between profit and loss.

Loss of a major contract

> When we bought Taunton Cider, our shareholders were also our largest customers. This enabled long-term supply contracts to be negotiated which providing a significant degree of commercial protection and stability, which was fundamental given the amount of debt being incurred. This is not always possible.

A business where sales are dominated by a relatively small number of customers has obvious advantages and drawbacks.

While large contracts being won and lost are a common feature of any commercial landscape, they can obviously represent a major threat to a fledgling MBO/MBI.

2. People

Business would be simple but for the people involved in it!

The team may have performed well on the deal but performing in the job is another matter. This is more likely to occur in an MBI where one or more members of the management team are new to the business.

Almost every company featured in the chapter *Real Deals* had significant problems caused by issues with people.

3. Failure of due diligence and the emergence of a black hole

This is not as uncommon as one might expect. Having talked with private equity managers, there are many examples of this happening.

This is less often the case with MBOs – for obvious reasons.

4. A dysfunctional and ineffective board

(As covered in an earlier chapter.)

Main drivers of success in MBOs/MBIs

Many books have been written on: *Winning Strategies, How to Be Successful, Crushing your Competitors, Doubling your Market Shares,* and so on. Obviously there is no panacea, otherwise no businesses would ever fail.

Having discussed this topic at length with venture capitalists, academics, advisors and management veterans, the factors listed below would appear to be the keys to success. If only we knew their relative importance!

1. The MBO/MBI will have **paid no more than a full price for the target company**. A leveraged financing structure is very rarely able to cope with the combined effect of the strain of a very full price and have the capacity to cope with shocks, which hit all businesses from time to time - no matter how able and talented the management team may be.

2. A **simple, competitive strategy** (one which meets the elevator test). Taunton Cider's MBO had a very simple strategy, understood by all five hundred employees – which is why 98% of them invested in the deal.

3. **Well-defined and well-understood company culture and values**.

4. **Well-organised and rigorous implementation process**. ("A good plan, violently executed now, is better than a perfect plan next week." General George S. Patton.)

5. **Comprehensive and understandable measurement of progress** against the vital objectives needs to be in place. Use of KPIs and a corporate dashboard philosophy. The introduction of *balanced scorecards* into Maybridge with the arrival of Nick Kerton, as the new CEO, paid dividends.

6. **Excellent communications** within the business and with all the stakeholders (customers, clients, equity investors, debt-providers, media, industry commentators, creditors and suppliers). Making full use of modern technology.

7. A **strong and mutually supportive management team**. There needs to be some surplus capacity to cope with the unexpected.

8. An **effective and well-run board**. A good balance and blend of executive and non-executive directors.

9. **Reliable, accurate management information** which focuses on the important issues.

10. **Accurate forecasting and projections**.

11. A serving, or two, of **good luck!**

The work-out situation

When the wheels come off

The *work-out*, also known as the *corporate recovery* or *turnaround*, situation is an industry in itself. It has its own industry association: The Association of Business Recovery Professionals. In this section I focus upon the effects on management in the context of an MBO/MBI.

There are many well-known companies which have experienced major difficulties, and have grappled with them in the goldfish bowl that is the plc arena: Bhs, Mothercare, Rover, J Sainsbury, WHSmith, British Airways, British Steel, Jarvis and Turner & Newell to name but a few. Smaller companies are just as likely to get into financial difficulty; data from business information specialist Dun and Bradstreet show that between 18,000–20,000 companies go bust each year.

No one knows how many company rescues and turnarounds there are each year, as it's not difficult to imagine that directors and shareholders prefer to keep this quiet. In fact there are major disadvantages in broadcasting your difficulties: it can trigger a tightening of terms by suppliers and other creditors, which piles on the pressure and reduce your chances of survival.

The Association of Business Recovery Professionals' sister association is the Society of Turnaround Professionals (STP), which supplies company doctors and other turnaround experts to assist companies in financial difficulties; it claims a relatively high success rate. Further, according to a London Business School survey, around 75% of all companies which go into bank supervision survive the course.

How does the situation arise?

It arises through underperformance against plan. In an MBO/MBI the leverage makes the position more difficult to manage. Prudent business plans allow for a degree of underperformance: 5-10% behind plan should be able to be accommodated within the company's facilities with the equity and debt providers.

Table 7.1: Performance 5-10% behind plan

Survivable	Business Plan	Actual	Comment
Turnover	100	95	Price concessions to major accounts
Variable costs	75	72	Aggressive buying of raw materials
Gross margin	25	23	Disappointing
Overheads	10	9	Cuts into fat but not muscle
EBIT	15	14	Almost there
Interest	10	10	Can't be reduced!
PBT	5	4	20% behind plan. Ouch!

A performance worse than the scenario above will cause significant problems.

Table 7.2: Performance more than 10% behind plan

Major problems	Business plan	Actual	Comment
Turnover	100	85	Price-war
Variable costs	75	70	Aggressive cost-reductions achieved
Gross margin	25	15	
Overheads	10	7	Cuts into muscle. Company on a 'war footing'.
EBIT	15	8	Almost halved
Interest	10	10	Can't be covered!
PBT	5	-2	A loss

The scenario above is entirely plausible and will probably be recognised by many businessmen. In a normal situation management would batten down the hatches and ride the storm out.

In an MBO/MBI this isn't always possible. Why? Because the VC and banks, who have backed the business, need their interest to be paid. Otherwise their financial returns will fall and, subsequently, so will the return they provide to their own shareholders and investors.

This scenario is a heady cocktail. The management team, who have experienced downturns in performance before, can be surprised by their new backers attitude which, depending on circumstances, can be anywhere on a spectrum from surprise and disappointment to complete sense of humour failure.

What happens?

The response will often depend on whether the news was expected or came as a bolt out of the blue. If board processes are working well and communications with investors is good, the setback may have been anticipated. Frequently, setbacks aren't seen coming and they strike without notice.

Investors generally do not like surprises, but investors in an MBO/MBI really hate surprises because they know the company's financing structure is not designed to withstand major shocks.

As the news spreads among the backers, they will want one question answered above all: 'Is this a one-off, or is the company on a different trajectory to the one we thought?'

As the management team you will probably already know the answer.

If it is a one-off, and performance returns to plan, then normal service will be resumed shortly.

If the wheels are coming off, the commercial world's equivalent of Alton Towers' 'Nemesis' ride beckons!

The right thing to do?

"Don't panic Mr Mainwaring!"

Corporal Jones in Dad's Army

Undoubtedly, recognising and accepting the business has a problem is a major first step. Just like alcoholics, boards can stay in denial for a long time.

> This was a feature of the Cloverleaf board as the year-end forecast was salami-sliced at successive monthly board meetings for quite a while.

Small businesses are often run by a strong owner-driver who refuses to accept the problem for what it is. Moreover, a trait of successful entrepreneurs is their durability and self-belief when times are tough. Whilst usually a great source of strength for the company, these factors can also work against fast recognition and acceptance of problems.

The need to act fast

Recovery professionals are unanimous on one thing: in a problematic situation it's never too soon to act, but it can be too late. Time is the sworn enemy of a failing business.

> The swift action by Bridgepoint's team at Dennis-Eagle probably averted a major problem being brought about by the receivership of some key suppliers and a severe short-term downturn in orders.

Generally, deteriorating performance seems to have a habit of gaining momentum and the business can tip into a tail-spin. This explains why the City usually sharply marks down the share price of a company in the wake of a profits warning; experience tells analysts that further profit warnings will probably follow.

The following tables provides some guidelines and questions the board should address and be aware of.

1. Immediate

Business receives shock with major impact.

Board	VC	Banks
Threat assessment Is this an acute or chronic problem? **Recovery plan** Prepare a plan to address the problem(s). Re-forecast for the next 3 months including weekly cash-flows. Prepare a hymn-sheet for consistent communications.	May provide an additional pair of hands to assist. VCs have different styles. Some are very hands-on and active, others are more passive.	Will 'sit on their hands and observe'. May put their work-out Department on notice.

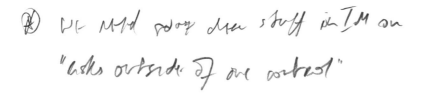

Ⓐ VC Md poor due stuff in IM on "risks outside of our control"

2. Up to four weeks

Initial shock absorbed but effect likely to be significant and long-term.

Board	VC	Banks
Refine recovery plan and begin implementation. Engage additional resources if needed. New business plan required.	Help and/or observe. Request information.	Observe. Ensure information is being provided. Ask for management presentation.

3. Up to three months

Short-term stability while threat is reassessed and view formed on future prospects.

Board	VC	Banks
Progress against revised business plan monitored closely. In-depth dealings with the banks' work-out team. More frequent board meetings.	Need to identify any 'new money' requirement. Terms of new money agreed. Negotiations with management and banks.	Credit committee insists work-out team appointed. Management informed. Work-out team complete exercise and report.

4. Up to twelve months

The refinancing phase, provided business is thought capable of trading through into calmer seas.

If trading-on is not thought possible, the insolvency phase is entered.

Board	VC	Banks
Management of all stakeholders' expectations. Form a view on whether the business can trade-through by running a major review. Be aware of exit opportunities. Insolvency advice.	May renegotiate terms of equity funding. Investment committee fully engaged. May seek management changes. Will decide whether to support the trading-through scenario or withdraw.	Will consider deferred repayment, but usually with conditions attached. Decide whether to support the recovery plan or withdraw via forced sale or appointment of administrator.

Identify the root cause

These tend to fall into three categories in the case of an MBO/MBI, but they are not mutually exclusive.

1. **A major one-off event**
   This is well-covered in Barbara Cassani's book *Go: An Airline Adventure*, which deals with the MBO. No sooner had this ground-breaking deal been completed than along came the tragedy of 9/11. The business subsequently stared into an abyss. Whatever the detailed causes, and there were many, the business faced extinction without strong and effective management action to increase revenues, cut costs, and improve cash flow and profits.

2. **Chronic underperformance** which traces to a failing business model or strategy.

   - Lost contract(s)

   - Competitive action

   - Cost and/or price movements

3. **A poor deal being struck**

   - Overpaying for the business

   - Failing to understand the business

   - Emergence of a black hole

Get external advice and input

There are specialists who have experience in these situations. A number of sources can introduce you to them:

- non-executive directors on your board;

- backers (the venture capitalist and bank will have contacts);

- accountants and auditors; and

- the internet (e.g. the Society of Turnaround Professionals, www.stp-uk.org).

> At Cloverleaf and Webb's Country Foods, we made extensive use of turnaround professionals who joined the boards – they made substantial contributions towards the recovery and the exits via trade sales of both companies.

Making the team work

Patrick Dunne of 3i makes the point that to succeed in a work-out situation the chairman and CEO must use all the resources available to them. The most capable leaders are able to motivate those around them and get the best out of their team. This can only increase a company's chances of trading–through.

A war footing

Short-term attitudes and priorities need to change. To achieve such changes of the type that may be necessary, some shocks may be required to convince colleagues and employees the situation is potentially serious. Some good examples are:

- recruitment freeze;

- cancellation of overnight stays for all managers;

- second class rail travel; and

- car-sharing.

These actions won't save much themselves; their real value is they might trigger a change in behaviour and outlook which will lead to some significant savings.

Key issues to be aware of

Being on the board of a company heading towards insolvency confers substantial responsibilities on the directors. The board should ensure it briefs its lawyers fully in order that they can issue detailed and specific advice. That said, this is no painting-by-numbers exercise, and directors will, on many occasions, have to use their judgement in making key decisions.

Tests of insolvency

In short, this is when a company can't pay its bills as they are due. Technically there are a couple of pure accountancy tests which are not entirely prescriptive but they serve as a guide:

- the **balance sheet test**: the company's liabilities exceed its assets; or

- the **going concern test**: the company is unable to pay its debts as they fall due. This is often referred to as the *cash flow* or *liquidity test*.

If the company is thought to be insolvent, or is in the *twilight zone* as it is sometimes called (or heading towards it), then other tests must be considered.

Wrongful trading

Wrongful trading occurs when the company continues trading when it can be argued there is no reasonable prospect of avoiding an insolvent liquidation. Further, in trading-on the directors may have exposed the company's creditors to greater losses.

When to stop trading

This isn't a black and white issue, hence the need for management's judgement. If it is judged to be clear that the company cannot realistically carry on, trading should cease so as to avoid further liabilities being incurred. It is the directors' duty to take every step to minimise losses to creditors.

However, in some circumstances it may be beneficial, from the creditors' perspective, for trading to continue. For example, to achieve a sale of the business as a going concern.

Whatever the board's decision, it, and the reasons it was reached, must be properly documented.

The decision to cease trading is achieved with the board (and the agreement of its backers) appointing an administrator, who effectively runs the company thereafter to a well prescribed process.

Disqualification proceedings

A director of a company which goes bust is liable to disqualification if his conduct is subsequently argued to be such as to make him unfit to be concerned in the future management of the company.

Who is at risk?

The answer is: not just the executive directors. Former directors and non-executive directors are at risk along with shadow directors. The latter may be consultants or senior managers who, it can be argued, were acting in a director's capacity or stead.

It is the responsibility of the liquidator, administrator or receiver to produce a confidential report to the DTI in respect of potential proceedings against directors. Matters which are likely to influence their report include:

- the scale of the insolvency;
- does the scale fit the scenario (i.e. is it substantially greater than it should have been);
- remaining value of assets and the nature of any preceding disposals;
- director's length of service;
- quality and integrity of financial records and board minutes; and
- views of creditors – how well were their interests protected?

The secretary of state or the official receiver may commence disqualification proceedings against the director. Proceedings must be commenced within two years of the date on which the company entered a formal insolvency procedure.

How to reduce exposure to liability?

As covered above, it is wrongful trading which poses the most serious risk to a director. Adherence to good practice will improve your position.

Good practice for directors

- You must have **accurate and timely management information.** Do not fly blind.

- Seek professional advice from lawyers, accountants and specialist insolvency practitioners (for the board and, in extremis, as an individual if he is at odds with colleagues).

- **Regular board meetings with accurate minutes.** The frequency of meetings may have to be increased to weekly, or even daily, with attendance by telephone for some members.

- **Consider carefully, and document, reasons for continuing to trade.** Cover off the creditors' interests and ensure you are treating them all fairly. You cannot favour any of them.

- **Avoid incurring additional liabilities** unless you have a very good reason for doing so (i.e. it will improve creditors prospects).

- **Resignation is unlikely to absolve a director of responsibility.** On the contrary, it could be argued the resignation could make things worse by destabilising the situation!

- **Regular and accurate communications with key stakeholders,** such as banks, credit insurers, leasing companies etc.

- **Keep up a dialogue with creditors** and attempt to work out a payments schedule with them. If you do – stick to it. You are not allowed to favour any creditors preferentially. This obviously requires very skilful handling as some, frankly, will be more important to the business than others.

- **Continually review your position and act accordingly.**

Preference

Another backwards looking test which needs to show that no one was discriminated against, positively or negatively. In particular, payments to directors need to be monitored carefully. Common sense would tell you that directors loans etc. could not be made; but trickier is the payment due to a director if the board had decided he should leave the company straight away.

Chapter 8

The MBO/MBI Scorecard

As covered in earlier chapters, the failure rate of MBOs and MBIs is high. I believe that the success rate can be improved with steps taken pre- and post-completion to identify potential weaknesses and flaws with the target company and its management. It is far easier to address weaknesses before completion than in its aftermath. Moreover, deferring problems can exacerbate them.

This chapter focuses upon a scorecard I have developed, which can form the basis of workshops with management teams to identify problems before they occur. It is no panacea for avoiding failure but it will improve the chances of success.

Criteria

1. Market
2. Competitive position
3. Marketing
4. Customers
5. Production
6. Distribution
7. IT and MIS
8. People
9. Financial record
10. Financing
11. Exit prospects
12. Other

1. Market

	Criteria	Comments
a	Growth prospects	Based on recent history, can growth be forecasted with confidence?
b	Profitability	Are major players in the market making good profits?
c	Competitive intensity	Are industry profits stable? Threats in the future?
d	Route to market	Effective or a bottle-neck?
e	Gross margin level	Enough to go around or dog-eat-dog?

This sets the scene for growth and your competitive position. A low score here should raise questions over the likelihood of being able to achieve sustainable growth.

2. Competitive position

	Criteria	Comments
a	Market share	Relative market share against the market leader?
b	Market leadership	Are you a market leader or follower?
c	5 year trend in market share	Are you gaining or losing share?
d	New entrants	Are new entrants likely to destabilise the market?

A simple but revealing section – no hiding place for a weak position. A low score can be partially offset by very strong market growth. A high score will probably be reflected in the price of the target company.

3. Marketing

	Criteria	Comments
a	Brand strength	Do you have brands or commodities?
b	Media expenditure	How significant is your level of brand support?
c	Media consistency	Are you supporting your brands consistently or as and when it can be afforded?
d	Success with NPD	Do products introduced in the last few years account for a significant proportion of turnover?
e	Creative strength	Do you have well-known advertising campaigns?
f	Promotion	Do they build customer trial and/or loyalty or are they surrogate price reductions?
g	Image	Do you have a positive or tarnished image for your products?

As a marketer by background, I'm bound to focus on this section! For a branded business a high score is essential. Commodity, or very price-sensitive, businesses need very strong scores in other sections to compensate for a low result here.

4. Customers

	Criteria	Comments
a	Number of major customers	Do you have a good spread or are you heavily reliant on a small number?
b	Quality of relations	Are relations with major customers harmonious or strained?
c	Trading history	Is trading with your major customers well-established or relatively recent?
d	Chairman and CEO contacts	Do you have effective senior relationships, or do you rely heavily on your sales management?
e	Knowledge of customers	Do you have a clean and well-used database, or is it a fog?
f	Service levels	Do you meaningfully measure and understand these, or are they guesstimated?
g	Customer satisfaction	Do you monitor these, and are complaints at an acceptable level?
h	Trade channel grip	Do you have a good level of control of your routes to market?

All businesses have customers. Low scores here should ring alarm bells. Customer referencing in due diligence will add some texture to this section.

5. Production

	Criteria	Comments
a	Supply chain	Is your supply chain robust, or is it fragile?
b	Production efficiency	Does production run smoothly, or is it running management ragged?
c	Capacity	Do you have adequate spare capacity (to meet your sales projections), or are you struggling to cope?
d	Cost of goods	Are these stable, or increasing?
e	Raw materials availability	Is this stable, predictable and plentiful, or is it difficult and unreliable?
f	Production sites – number	Do you operate from a single well-ordered site, or do you have several disparate ones?
g	Production sites – quality	Are your production sites clean, environmentally sound and secure, or a do you have a 'few issues'?
h	Quality of capital	Are your manufacturing assets modern and up to date, or are they 'knackered'?

Under-capitalised production sites always cause problems, if only because significant capex will usually be required. This needs cash and MBOs/MBIs are usually short of it. The Maybridge and Cloverleaf stories highlight issues here. Cost of goods is a key factor too – it almost sank Webb's Country Foods.

6. Distribution

	Criteria	Comments
a	Costs	Are these costs small or substantial in relation to turnover?
b	In-house/contracted out	Do you add value by manufacturing in-house, or should you be contracting-out?
c	Control of warehousing/logistics	Do you have solid and professional control, or is it frankly abdicated?

Customers are intolerant of poor service levels, and a highly leveraged MBO/MBI will struggle to withstand the loss of significant chunks of turnover. Contracting-out can be a double-edged sword: if it works, it is very cost-effective; if it goes wrong, for reasons outside your control, it can have devastating repercussions.

7. IT and MIS

	Criteria	Comments
a	Modernity	Do you have leading edge technology and systems, or quill pens and candles?
b	Website	Is this really effective?
c	Communications	Are you using modern technology to achieve good communications, or are you still printing off emails?
d	Robustness of system	Are your systems effective and reliable, or continually falling over?

Because of the need for accurate and timely information this is key. Ashford Colour Press suffered from failure in this area initially. Backers are unforgiving if you are flying blind for anything other than a very short period.

8. People

	Criteria	Comments
a	Principals' preparedness	Do you understand and are you, individually and severally, prepared for the demands of an MBO/MBI?
b	Management track record	Are you a well-proven and settled team, or 'newly-weds'?
c	Good board/ bad board	Is your board truly effective, or a fuddled bureaucracy?
d	Absence rates	Are these above or below the industry norms?
e	Staff turnover	Do you have a history of 'stayers', or more of a revolving door?
f	Equity involvement for senior management	Will all those managers, who will determine your success or failure, be adequately incentivised?

The reason why most acquisitions fail, says conventional wisdom! A low score here should raise serious questions. Bad boards wreck businesses.

9. Financial record

	Criteria	Comments
a	5 year sales	Can you display consistent year on year growth, or is it lumpy?
b	5 year margins	Are your margins trending up, flat or down?
c	Current net margin	10% is a good average. Above that is likely to be unsustainable. 5% is too low.
d	Cash generation	This is your company's lifeblood – how strongly and consistently do you generate it?
e	Debtors	Do most major customers pay on time, or do you have some taking over 90 days?
f	Creditors	Do you have a good payment record, or have you stretched several too far?
g	Price increases	Can you still achieve these, or are they a fading memory?

Obviously important, and the easiest area to check and verify. Due diligence will test this to destruction. A low score here and your deal is holed below the water-line. Think very carefully before proceeding.

10. Financing

	Criteria	Comments
a	Probable price	Are you likely to have to pay a high or low price to acquire your target company?
b	Senior debt availability	Do you have good asset backing against which to borrow funds?
c	Management equity	What is your appetite and ability to invest in this deal?
d	Ability to withstand due diligence	Will the business withstand its 'full structural survey', or are skeletons likely to be found?

Another key area as a main cause of MBO/MBI failure is when too high a price is paid.

11. Exit prospects

	Criteria	Comments
a	Possible trade buyers	Can you see trade buyers for your business in two or three years?
b	Flotation prospects	What are your prospects of achieving a flotation?
c	History of M&A in market	Have there been successful deals in your market in recent times, or any notable failures?
d	Acquisitions	Will you need to acquire further businesses to achieve your business plan?

This issue will arise fairly early on in the MBO/MBI process with potential backers. Venture capital is like air under pressure: it will always be trying to seek an exit, so it's important there are some realistic options.

12. Other

	Criteria	Comments
a	Cost savings potential	Is there low-hanging fruit to go after, or has the business been too well-managed already?
b	Ability to sell other products through distribution channels	Can you sell other goods and/or services in the future without expanding your sales resource?
c	Overseas potential	Do you have real potential here, or is it more likely a recipe for bad debts and stock write-offs?
d	Vendor vacuum	Can you fill the vacuum left as your vendor withdraws?
e	Black hole possibility	Do you have any fears over a 'black-hole' being discovered beyond completion?

Some key criteria here. Vendor vacuum is a potentially fatal flaw unless it is identified and fully planned for. Black holes are another well-known elephant trap. Maybridge and Webb's Country Foods display these problems vividly.

Table 8.1: Guide to scoring

KEY	1	2	3	4	5
Score	Very negative	Negative	Neutral	Positive	Very positive
Weighting	Unimportant	Significant	Crucial		

The scorecard divides a business up into several key areas and gives a guide to the various issues to be scored in each. A simple weighting ascribed to the criteria then builds a composite score. Thanks to Excel the results can be quickly graphed.

In the *Real Deals* chapter each of the seven companies has been put through the process and scored. The analysis shows some very interesting variations and, not surprisingly, there is a correlation between the results achieved on the scorecard and the ultimate degree of success achieved by the MBO/MBI.

Chapter 9

Real Deals

The previous chapter explained how a scorecard can improve chances of success by highlighting a company's strengths and potential weaknesses. This chapter covers the journey of seven companies through the deal itself and towards, and in most cases through, the exit.

It's abundantly clear from the analysis that we can do more than employ twenty-twenty hindsight vision. Objective analysis carried out pre-completion can identify potential problems and relative weaknesses. Once identified these should be squarely confronted and resolved.

Scorecard results

Table 9.1: MBO/MBI scorecard for the seven real deals

Real deal company	Total score
Taunton Cider	576
Ashford Colour Press	535
Dennis-Eagle	465
Cloverleaf	350
Maybridge	459
Tubex	500
Webb's	341

Figure 9.1: MBO/MBI scorecard for the seven real deals

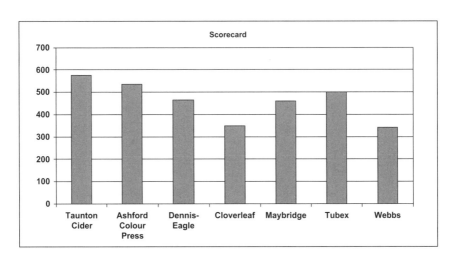

Taunton Cider Ltd 1991-1996

A great success – the MBO wins the auction and proceeds to flotation in fourteen months, achieving a forty times increase in value for shareholders.

Background and milestones

Taunton Cider had its origins in the 19th century. It was registered as a limited company in 1921, and in the 1960s the business expanded as Courage and Bass decided to pool their cider interests and create a stronger competitor to Bulmers. As the company gained momentum, so other brewers were attracted. Guinness joined the consortium in 1972 and brought with them their marketing tool kit. Dry Blackthorn was created as a mainstream brand, and was launched nationally as the first *dry* cider on draught.

By the mid-1980s the firm accounted for a quarter of the UK's cider market, and products were introduced into the take-home market. The market had been expanding since the early 1930s, and was about to achieve explosive growth as marketing strategies sought to change the consumers' image of the product from west country rocket fuel to a more contemporary and stylish long drink. The task was to encourage consumers to see cider as *beer made from apples.* Further, the apple base provided the opportunity to make a wide range of products varying in taste, strength and appearance.

In 1990, the Monopolies and Mergers Commission report concluded that the UK's brewing industry was a "complex monopoly". As a result the main shareholders of Taunton Cider decided to divest their out-riding businesses, to allow them to focus on the structural change which was now indicated in their core activities.

The Taunton Cider board was instructed to prepare the company for sale, and Schroders were appointed to handle the auction.

The MD, Peter Adams (not a chap to take a challenge lying down), set off at break-neck speed to find backers for a potential MBO. Brian Longstaff (the operations director) and yours truly (the commercial director) were to be joint principals in the potential deal. The FD was approaching retirement and was not invited into the deal. This seemed like a cruel act at the time but unquestionably proved to be the right decision. An interim finance director was brought on board from our auditors, to cope with the financial workload necessary to both produce information for the information memorandum and also to facilitate the MBO.

What I knew about MBOs/MBIs at that time could have been written on the back of a beer mat. What I didn't know would have filled a library. It was to be a very steep learning curve over the next six months.

Our major shareholders were sceptical about the putative MBO. At that time the market was relatively immature and deals of the size we were contemplating was leading-edge territory. They were concerned we would become distracted to the detriment of achieving a trade sale of their business.

Backers

Samuel Montagu, then HSBC's merchant banking arm, won the beauty parade of corporate advisors and were appointed by management as the ring masters. They introduced Morgan Grenfell Development Capital (MGDC) as equity providers, who were at the time under Robert Smith and Norman Murray, known as an effective and somewhat feisty firm. Their track record suggested they were straightforward operators who weren't afraid of the unconventional. They got deals done. The debt financing was provided by Samuel Montagu, and the Midland bank retained the day-to-day clearing functions. Accountants were Coopers and Lybrand, already our auditors, and our London lawyers, Nicholson Graham & Jones, completed the team.

Equity

MGDC led the equity investors but, because of the size of the deal, it was syndicated to CINVEN and Midland Montagu. Additionally, a mezzanine strip (debt with an in-built equity kicker) was put in place.

Debt

Facilities of £59m comprised of term and revolving debt were agreed, to provide the necessary facilities.

Highlights and lessons

An MBO can win even the most keenly contested auction.

Schroders oversaw the preparation of the information memorandum and, following its circulation, Round 1 bidders were duly presented to. Schroders rode shotgun on all of these to ensure a level playing field. The major shareholders came to realise that we were becoming deadly serious about launching an MBO, and agreed that our bid could be submitted at the end of Round 1 – which it duly was, with a degree of trepidation.

The workload was crushing. We still had the day-to-day business to run, which was expanding fast as new brands Diamond White, Diamond Blush and Red Rock ("It's not red and there are no rocks in it" said

> Wide distribution of the sweet equity galvanised and focused the entire management team.

Leslie Nielsen on the TV ads) generated unprecedented growth. We also had to do our utmost to sell the business to trade buyers, as well as to persuade the MBO backers that this was a deal with potential.

In addition to the three directors who were principals, the senior management team was positively engaged. They were kept up to date on developments, and setbacks, with frequent meetings. An early promise of equity involvement proved to be a significant motivator and provided the cohesiveness when it was needed.

This is the meeting, at the end of the due diligence process, when the indicative offer needs to become a firm one. If the price is to be reduced, this is where it will happen: emotions can run high, as they did in this case!

The meeting was an education. Unaware of what was to come we attended a meeting, at Schroders offices, of the entire MBO team with our advisors and the same complement from the vendor's

> Venture capitalists aimed to reduce the initial indicative offer, based on findings from the due diligence process.

side. Norman Murray was there alongside the irrepressible pair of Gough and Weston. We sensed trouble! After the initial pleasantries, which didn't take long as I recall, battle commenced. Morgan Grenfell Development Capital's team had decided to reduce the price to be paid and set about convincing the other side. The trouble was the other side had their own heavyweights in Nick Bryan and Tony Portno, and they saw it coming.

There ensued a ritual dance, with parties coming and going from the room like an Ealing farce. We three principals of the deal were merely an accessory for the meeting, watching swivel-headed, as though at Wimbledon, concerned as our dream of completion repeatedly came into focus only to fade again, as the arguments raged. Many people were crossed off each others Christmas card list that day.

The price was reduced – but not by much.

Completion achieved in a full-blown recession

We worked through a very long and depressing winter. In 1991, the first Gulf war broke out and the economy was diving headlong into full-blown recession. The main benefit of this was that most London hotels were empty and we camped at the Hampshire, in Leicester Square, on modest bed and breakfast rates. Our days were filled with endless meetings negotiating contracts with: our major customers (these were *condition precedents* for the deal, as our main customers were also our main shareholders); main suppliers and creditors; equity and debt providers and our legal team. The drafting meetings were also interminable as literally every word was scrutinised and verified to the satisfaction of all concerned.

In May 1991 we finally completed the deal. Many thought we were stark raving mad to have effectively borrowed £100m in the teeth of a recession. There were times when I was tempted to agree with them. We all experienced 'bolt-upright' moments in the middle of the night, as the serpents of doubt coiled in our guts. Fortunately, our senior management team had performed admirably while we were focused on the deal, and the business continued to increase sales, margins and profits.

Board matters

Composition

Michael Cottrell, an ex Courage Ltd MD, was appointed chairman, and MGDC appointed Jeremy Gough and Norman Murray as non-executive directors. They brought considerable experience and energy to the board. The three executive directors were later joined by a new and talented finance director, Nick Pearch. It was an excellent team and a very supportive atmosphere. This was just as well as our first two months trading nose-dived against plan as the UK suffered the wettest early summer in living memory. In July the sun shone and the anticipated growth returned – much to everyone's relief.

Good Board/Bad Board

The Taunton Cider board was strong and very well run.

- Board papers were extremely well presented. We had designed a pictorial pack which focused everyone on the important issues. The use of graphs also demystified the dreaded banking covenants and cash projections, which were critical to success.
- Debate was encouraged by the chairman and, while robust at times, never descended to the personal.
- Separate strategy boards were badged and well prepared for.
- Meetings rarely lasted more than three hours.

Strategy

Our strategy was simple and met the *elevator test.*

Roman legions taught us that 500 people is the optimum size for any organisation involved in human endeavour – and so it proved at Taunton Cider. Regular strategy and results briefings were organised, where the board would brief all employees in sessions staggered throughout a day at the village hall (Taunton Cider was based at Norton Fitzwarren, a village just to the west of Taunton). These were as well received as any I can remember in my career.

Running a business is 20% strategy and 80% implementation. Taunton Cider's management were very strong on implementation.

Performance

Bull points

- The innovative marketing strategies deployed succeeded in making consumers reappraise cider, and consequently delivered strong and consistent growth.

- We were winning consumers and the trade over to the new cider imagery.

- Bulmers looked on from the sidelines and saw their market share eroded as distribution and rate of sale gains drove our market share up towards 35%. In value market share (as against volume market share) terms we were breathing down their necks.

- Employees' support and commitment. 98% of all employees invested their own cash in the MBO, which had a galvanising effect.

- Performance pulled progressively ahead of plan, and profits and cash were so strong we were able to consider, and begin to plan, the exit within six months of completion of the MBO.

Bear points

- Could the explosive growth be maintained? It looked too good to be true.

- We were losing market share to Bulmers in the draught sector. Their competitive tactics were commoditising the sector.

Success or failure

The MBO of Taunton Cider was an unqualified success. A number of factors combined to achieve this.

- **Simple business strategy**, well-implemented.
- **Growing sales, healthy margins, excellent customer service and reliable supply-chain.**
- **Strong and growing brands.**
- An **effective and experienced board.**
- **Management nettles were grasped** and the necessary changes were made swiftly.

The exit

Rationale

'A bird in the hand' summarised our thinking. Growth in sales and profits had continued an established five year trend. The only argument for delay was the prospect of a higher price on flotation.

What happened

Within months of achieving completion on the MBO we were back in our City haunts planning the flotation on the Main Market.

There was a substantial workload involved, but the freshness of information and due diligence from the MBO reduced the amount of spade work required. While a flotation is a demanding process, compared to the unique exigencies of the MBO, it was relatively straight forward.

Taunton Cider was admitted to the Main Market in July 1992 to the amazement of many onlookers. At the time it was one of the most successful ever MBOs.

Results for stakeholders

The consideration paid for the company on the MBO was £72.5m. The business was floated for £156m – achieving a near **forty times growth in value of the sweet equity**. The performance ratchet on the management's share of the sweet equity was triggered at the top of its range.

Epilogue

Growth continued and results in the first year as a plc were above expectations; the share price rose towards £2 from the flotation price of £1.40.

All good things, it seems, come to an end sooner or later. Growth slowed and competition intensified which reduced margins and put profits under pressure. The drinks market continued to re-structure and consolidate; it was becoming increasingly clear that we were too big to hide and too small to run, as acquisitive drinks companies began to circle us.

Matthew Clark Ltd were pursuing a very aggressive buy-and-build strategy in the drinks market, focusing on wholesaling and branded alcoholic drinks. In 1994 they beat us to the punch and acquired the number three cidermaker, Gaymers Ltd, from Allied Domecq plc. Taunton Cider and Matthew Clark had the same chairman but, given they had now become a direct competitor, he had to decide which horse to ride. He elected to join Matthew Clark as he had been with them longer than with us. From that point on, we knew it was only a matter of time before they turned their attention towards us, to consolidate their position in the still buoyant cider market.

The overtures began in 1995 and, with the City firmly behind their buy-and-build strategy, they made their move. Fortunately our performance was still such that we were able to drive the bid price up, in return for a positive recommendation from our board to Taunton Cider shareholders.

In the autumn of 1995, a recommended offer of £280m was accepted, our senior team was dismantled and they asserted control.

However, it became increasingly apparent in 1996 that Matthew Clark had bitten off more than it could chew. The integration of Gaymers still hadn't been achieved, and the addition of Taunton Cider into the mix proved a step too far. Group profits disappointed the City, and in the wake of profit warnings the company flipped from a darling to being perceived as a basket case. Despite earlier written assurances that Taunton Cider's production base would be maintained at Norton Fitzwarren, the Matthew Clark board decided to cut its losses and consolidate production at the Shepton Mallett facility.

Matthew Clark's management were unable to recover from their setbacks and were later acquired by a large, private American company – the price achieved for the entire group was less than they had paid for Taunton Cider a few years previously.

Figure 9.2: MBO/MBI scorecard for Taunton Cider

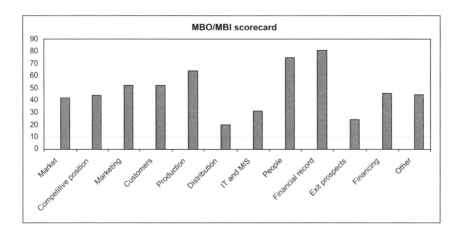

Tubex Ltd

A strong start, then progress stalled when a price war erupted with the previous owner's new company. Board changes were followed by a secondary MBO.

Tubex was formed by Graham Hurlstone in the early 1990s and based in Aberaman, near Merthyr Tydfil, in the Cynon Valley. The location was attractive due to the availability of skilled labour and grants from the government keen to attract manufacturing industries.

Tubex makes tree shelters. Now you have read this you will suddenly notice them everywhere! They are the biodegradable tubes saplings are planted in to protect them from hungry, small animals, and promote their growth in a mini-greenhouse type environment. The product was very effective – achieving a payback for the grower who could be persuaded to make the initial investment. The development of the products was a stroke of genius, as it transformed a producer of commoditised plastic extrusions into an added-value branded business. The business had achieved impressive and develop profitable growth in the UK and parts of Europe, and the founder decided to cash-in and retire.

The *value-play* for the MBI team was to de-seasonalise the business by selling existing products to woodland management in the southern hemisphere, and new products aimed at offering similar benefits to viticulturists.

Backers

- **Equity** was provided by NatWest Development Capital (now Bridgepoint Capital), and syndicated to 3i.

- **Debt** was provided via a factoring agreement with HSBC.

Highlights and lessons

Two MBI professionals take a risk

The business was acquired as an MBI by Peter Lee, a highly experienced managing director with strong production and operations credentials, and Nigel Skinner, a partner from Price Waterhouse. They held management's slice of the equity between them. While this is commonplace in many deals, in this instance it was to prove problematic.

A branded business is formed from a commoditised producer of plastics

The transition from being a producer of commoditised extruded plastic products to a manufacturer of branded goods was truly impressive. The business initially achieved growth and attractive margins. The progress of the deal is given below.

1. *The original vendor re-enters the market – the vendor's boomerang.*
    In 1999 the vendor decided to come out of retirement and aimed to repeat his success with a new company, Arbeta Ltd.

2. *A key Tubex director defects to his former boss's start-up.*
    The technical director decided, for a promise of wealth generation which had eluded him at Tubex, to jump ship and throw his lot in once again with Graham Hurlstone.

3. *A price war stalls progress.*
    The creation of a new and respected competitor in the UK, the engine room of profit for Tubex, caused a price war to break out. Tubex lost sales, with margin, profit and momentum all suffering. It had to swing into cost-reduction mode, and all the attendant problems associated with cutting into the muscle of the business arose.

4. *Excess supply as mother nature intervenes.*
    A near hurricane in northern France destroyed vast areas of woodland and, subsequently, supply swamped demand. This caused timber prices to fall and discouraged further planting. Demand for Tubex's woodland products was adversely affected.

5. *Demand is reduced by government cutbacks.*
    Government cuts in road-building programmes reduced the number of landscaping projects in the UK. The woodland management and commercial landscaping companies cut their cloth accordingly.

6. *Management changes meet the CEO's personal plans and momentum is restored.*
    In 2000, Peter Lee decided to hand over the CEO's position to Nigel Skinner in order to ease himself into semi-retirement and establish a non-executive portfolio. The board was re-structured; Lee became a non-executive director and retained his equity interest, and I took the chair.

Board matters

Composition

In addition to the principals, who became CEO and finance director, the senior team comprised technical director Mark Potter, and production director Andre Green. Later, a marketing manager, Andrew Binnie, was appointed. I joined the board in 1997, having been introduced by Chris Allner of NatWest Equity Partners.

Good board/bad board

The boards were well-prepared and well-run. Management information was exemplary.

Strategy

1. To sell existing woodland products to new customers and develop new products for a new market in viticulture.
2. The Tubex brand was to be developed and offer new services (e.g. advice on woodland management).

Performance

Bull points

- Initial performance in 1997 was above plan.
- The efficiency of production and operations was improved.
- The business increased profits and generated significant cash.
- Marketing plans were implemented.
- The new viticulture products were successful, gaining distribution and significant sales.
- Competitive intensity was low, and Tubex had erected barriers to entry with their scale of economies and technical knowledge.
- Equity-based incentives were introduced for the three new executive directors who joined the board in 2000. The strengthened Tubex board gelled into an effective team.

- The ability and dexterity of Tubex's management produced significant cost-savings, enabling it to trade-through the downturn within its banking facilities.

- Investors remained steadfastly supportive.

- An imaginative refinancing, using the value of the freehold site, facilitated a secondary MBO.

Bear points

- A vendor's boomerang can be very damaging. Arbeta gained turnover but never made a profit. It only succeeded in destabilising the market.

- The allocation of the sweet equity in 1997 proved to be very divisive. It's doubtful the vendor would have re-entered the market if the technical director had been incentivised.

- Building a business overseas took longer than anticipated – doesn't it always, many would say.

- Overseas agents need to be managed closely.

Success or failure

- The original MBO did not achieve its original objectives as market conditions became severe.

- The achievement by management of coping with the consequences of a UK price war by aggressive cost reduction was impressive.

- Management of working capital to stay within the company's banking facilities was excellent.

- The refinancing to achieve the secondary MBO, and consequently an increase in value for Bridgepoint, was undoubtedly a success.

The exit

- In 2001, a secondary MBO was explored. The structure of the original MBO was such that, over time, the running yield was increasing and the drain on operating cashflow was beginning to hurt. The original deal structure was doing what it was supposed to do (i.e. tighten a noose and encourage the management team to exit).

- Shareholders recognised this and were supportive of management's intentions.

- There was strength in the balance sheet from the freehold on the manufacturing site. The plan was to organise a sale and leaseback to release the cash and so facilitate a re-financing.

- This was achieved, and Bridgepoint achieved their exit as the equity in *newco* was shared between 3i and management.

- Bridgepoint exited happily and 3i and management achieved a greater share of equity. The factoring arrangement was renewed with HSBC.

Epilogue

I exited with Bridgepoint, as the secondary MBO completed, and handed over to a new chairman.

In 2002, Tubex put Arbeta out of its agony and acquired it as a going concern for a modest consideration. The combined company has consolidated its UK position, and this has allowed it to refocus on overseas growth.

Significant trading success has been achieved subsequently, and sales and profits have increased.

Figure 9.3: MBO/MBI scorecard for Tubex Ltd

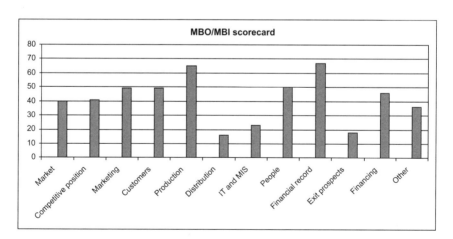

Maybridge plc

 A clash of cultures, coupled with an <u>over-optimistic original business plan</u>, caused major problems. Management changes and a well-implemented new business strategy, brought success and a trade sale.

Background and milestones

A family business, established in 1962, and run by Dr Roden Bridgewater. He set the business up after he left an American pharmaceutical corporation and returned to the UK.

The company was established on the site of an old quarry in Tintagel, to make and sell heterocyclic compounds to chemists in agricultural chemicals and pharmaceuticals. The location on Cornwall's beautiful north coast was a draw for chemists seeking a higher quality of life. Moreover, since the weight in kilos of annual turnover in £20 notes was considerably greater than the weight of the actual product shipped from the plant (products were sold by the milligram), distribution costs were almost an irrelevance.

These products are used by pharmaceutical, and more recently biotechnology companies, to assist them in various stages of the difficult process of drug development. Maybridge had no equity interest in the development of its customers' drugs – it merely sells its unique compounds for cash.

The original business strategy was to recruit chemists (who were targeted to bring in 3.5 times their cost in sales), and it took until 1990 to achieve total annual sales of £1m. Working conditions were somewhat rudimentary, and the company's culture could be described as quirky and hierarchical.

From the initial period of gradual sales development came the boom of the early 1990s. This was caused by the mapping of the human genome, which led to the formation of the biotechnology sector with research and development funds to burn. There was also the fact that traditional pharmaceutical companies, suffering from a lack of new products, significantly stepped up demand for diverse screening compounds of the type made by Maybridge.

Several UK companies were backed by venture capitalists and achieved flotation onto the London Stock Exchange. One such example was Oxford Diversity, which achieved a notable success for 3i.

Maybridge continued to increase annual turnover towards the £5m level, but family health problems started to tell on the owner. Meanwhile, 3i were looking for the next Oxford Diversity, and Maybridge was identified as a target company.

Dr Roger Newton, an internationally renowned chemist, was retained by 3i to review the company. Subsequently a plan for a BIMBO was prepared and, after a limited auction, a deal was completed with Roden Bridgewater in 1997. The company was a thriving small business by this time, but the shareholders were looking for significant additional growth. Company culture was about to receive something of a shock!

The early days were very tough for a variety of reasons, including a difficult working relationship between Roger Newton (who was appointed part-time CEO) and the long-serving chief chemist at Maybridge. The marriage of new and old management soon found itself headed for the Cornish rocks.

Bill Hiscocks, of 3i, and I were appointed to the board as non-executive directors after completion.

Initially it was like swimming in treacle. The clashes between the new and old management styles continued, and the company under-achieved against its business plan. 3i and the bank started to become nervous. Despite huge efforts by the recently appointed finance director, Les Eastlake, management information was sparse and inconsistent and we were in thick fog for most of 1998.

After twelve months of underperformance it was obvious change was required. Roger Newton's substantial commitments elsewhere meant he simply couldn't become full-time. At 3i's behest, I stepped up to chairman and Roger Newton's role was re-shaped, becoming vice-chairman and focusing on areas where he could really add value (i.e. with leading-edge chemistry and building new relationships with other cognoscenti in the drug discovery world). He designed new added-value compounds which sold at premium prices. New manufacturing partnerships were struck which radically increased productivity and cut lead-times. He also formed the first joint ventures for the business.

In 1999, Bill Hiscocks moved to Singapore to run 3i's operations, and Roger Lawson, a highly experienced 3i veteran, came aboard.

Sadly, the former chief chemist, Bernie Bull, who latterly began to enjoy life at the company again, as he could see real progress was being made at last, suffered a major heart attack and was unable to continue in the business and had to step down from the team and retire. We made the decision to bring in a full-time CEO. The search found the highly talented Dr Nick Kerton, a PhD chemist, natural leader and marketer, who was to prove instrumental in transforming the company's fortunes.

Following Nick Kerton's arrival, strategy was overhauled and the business was completely reorganised. Conventional production, operations and marketing disciplines were introduced, several staff changes were made and new finance and IT systems were installed. These changes, which took almost two years, achieved the modernisation which was desperately needed. Sales began to increase, boosted by new, well-packaged and marketed products, and customer service levels improved. Maybridge started to realise its potential and began to make serious money.

Backers

* Equity provided by 3i.

* Debt financing provided by the Royal Bank of Scotland.

Highlights and lessons

1. *A typical BIMBO. Strains between old and new management presented a real challenge.*
   The clash of the old and new management styles was counter-productive. It was like swimming in treacle.

2. *A black hole appeared which made matters worse.*
   A black hole appeared in the guise of very poor customer service levels. Fulfilment of orders was substantially worse than had been thought. When improved management information cast light on this aspect of the business, the results revealed were very poor.

3. *The changes that were necessary took longer than anticipated – they always seem to!*
   The main catalysts for achieving real change was focusing Roger Newton on premium product development and global networking with customers, and the appointment of the new CEO Nick Kerton.

4. *The revised strategy was successful.*

   Sales of nearly £10m were achieved in the year prior to the sale in 2002, with a PBIT in excess of 20% of sales.

5. *The original business plan proved unrealistic.*

   It had to be completely re-cast and new plans designed and implemented.

Board matters

Composition

- Andy Nash, Iain Macritchie: chairmen

- Roger Newton: CEO/vice chairman

- Nick Kerton: CEO

- Les Eastlake: finance director

- Bill Hiscocks, Roger Lawson: 3i non-executive directors

- Good board: overall functioned well as a team.

- 3i and RBS became very demanding due to sustained underperformance in the first two years.

Strategy

1. The **revised strategy**, agreed in March 2000, laid the foundations for success.

2. The **business model** changed from being production-pushed to demand-led.

3. More effective **premium products** were produced cost-effectively and professionally marketed to customers world-wide.

4. **Production facilities** were dramatically improved with investment in capacity and quality.

5. The **basic fabric of the business** received significant investment and was modernised.

Performance

Bull points

- The new managerial talent brought in transformed the business. This turned imminent failure into a substantial success. Untapped talent within the business flourished under the new leadership and vastly improved environment.

- The *Chemistry Factory* was reorganised with separate teams focusing on discrete product sectors. Significant capital expenditure increased output and margins.

- The quality of the working environment for everyone on site was improved dramatically (including: canteen, parking, security, PCs and office design).

- Improved compounds were marketed very efficiently by the beefed-up sales force (comprising mainly PhD chemists).

- Product awareness and demand were increased with internet-based marketing (including: website, online purchasing and tele-marketing).

- The 100 days taken to prepare a revised business plan delivered success in 1,000 days – sticking with the plan paid dividends.

- Customer service was completely transformed from *quill pens and candles* to a customer friendly internet-based system.

Bear points

- The original MBO/MBI structure was flawed.

- The initial business plan was too optimistic.

- The old culture wasn't capable of achieving profitable growth and tolerated weak performers.

- The chemistry production was random. Output was often at the whim of what the chemist working at the bench fancied making. He might have been in the mood to attempt to produce the chemical equivalent of a beef wellington, when what was needed by customers happened to be a boiled egg.

- The site was inefficient, following a sustained period of underinvestment in several management systems.

- The working environment in parts of the site was at best rudimentary.

Success or failure

- The initial plan, upon which the MBO/MBI deal was based, was too ambitious.

- The revised business plan targets, based on the 2000 strategy, were achieved.

- The visibility, strategic attraction and value of the business was significantly increased within the industry.

The exit

- By 2002, 3i were keen to crystallise value in an ageing investment.

- The company was privately marketed to a list of likely acquirers, and a trade sale was achieved to a company with a substantial commercial presence in the major international markets.

- The price achieved substantial value for equity holders.

Epilogue

The business is now subsumed within Fischer Scientific Inc.

Nick Kerton stayed with the business for the first year to help achieve integration, then left amicably having handed over to Fischer's management.

Figure 9.4: MBO/MBI scorecard for Maybridge plc

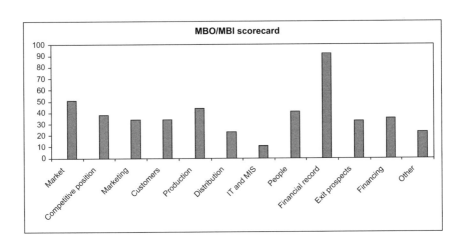

Webb's Country Foods Ltd

The inability of a leveraged structure to cope with a trading downturn, coupled with vendor vacuum, almost led to receivership. But management changes, cost reduction and excellent working capital resulted in a trade sale. Equity was restored to value with an innovative property deal.

Background and milestones

Webb's Country Foods Ltd was one of the UK's prominent processors of fresh chicken. It supplied stores' own label branded goods to several of the UK's major grocery chains. It also had an emerging business in the prepared meals and food service sector.

It was a sizeable enterprise, employing around 2,000 people at six manufacturing sites around the Midlands and southern England. The company was established by Leigh Webb, and had been a very strong and traditionally run business.

Poultry is a very cash generative business, albeit with a slim gross margin. Value-added processes in manufacturing are limited.

However the *Sunday Times Rich List* often features people from the UK poultry industry. The evidence was there to see – if you ran a tight ship, there was gold to be found amongst all those giblets.

In 1997, 3i backed an MBO which won the auction run at the behest of the vendor. The price was a full one, but could be justified if the growth strategy was achieved.

Given the size of the deal, 3i appointed three non-executive directors: Roger Lawson, a well-known 3i veteran; Bruce Purgavie, recently retired from Heinz, and I became chairman.

Backers

- **Equity** was provided by 3i. It wasn't syndicated. Barclays Capital provided mezzanine finance.
- **Debt** financing was provided by Barclays, Fortis and Rabobank.

Highlights and lessons

1. *A keenly contested auction led to a full price being paid.*

    The auction was keenly contested, as, given the growth achieved in the business and its relatively high margins compared to other chicken processors, the story was a good one.

2. *The management team was experienced but missed the vendor's driving force.*

    Management team comprised: Howard Gallagher, the previous operations director, who was appointed managing director on completion; Brian Taylor was the finance director; and David Price the marketing and sales director. Brian Watkins, who was to play a star role later, was company secretary.

3. *Mother nature defeats a leveraged structure.*

    A leveraged structure simply wasn't able to cope with a normal cyclical downturn in an agricultural business.

4. *Cash-starved companies struggle to reduce costs.*

    Reducing costs, in a very labour intensive business, inevitably means reducing headcount. This requires cash to fund redundancies. We didn't have the cash, and the backers were understandably very reluctant to provide it. It was the *throwing good money after bad* scenario.

5. *Professional work-out management pays huge dividends.*

    Somehow, Peter Walton, the interim managing director, managed to generate sufficient headroom out of working capital management to begin to rationalise the production and overhead base. It was the commercial equivalent of the biblical feeding of the five thousand. Two factories were closed and commercial activities were refocused onto the more profitable core areas.

6. *Delivering on revised targets rebuilt the backers confidence.*

    Communication with the backers was very good. Frequent presentations on progress were well-prepared and we earned respect by being straightforward, uncomplicated and delivering on revised targets.

7.   *Touch and go through the work-out phase.*

Barclays, on behalf of the banking syndicate, initiated a full *investigating accountants* report by Andersen's. It confirmed our hypothesis that the company was powerless to influence market-wide price reductions and cost increases. The best way out for backers was to support the management team, who were performing miracles to avoid insolvency, until market forces granted us salvation by bringing demand and supply back into equilibrium.

Board matters

Composition was the three non-execs, the three executive directors and the company secretary.

Good board/bad board

The board functioned reasonably well. In the early days, getting information proved to be quite a problem as the management information system was in its infancy. The previous owner was said to regard the bank statements as the most valuable performance indicator – and how right he was proved!

Strategy

The strategy was to achieve growth by working closely with the major grocery chains on a *category management* approach to the sector. This was to include in-depth involvement with the multiples' in-store investment in rotisseries. Additional growth would be achieved from the emerging food services sector (sandwich fillings), and the prepared meals' sector.

Performance

Bull points

- There weren't any bull points in the early stages!

- We avoided going bust by the skin of our teeth.

- Peter Walton, a work-out professional, was appointed interim CEO and brought the skills and disciplines to bear which were needed to manage a business in this situation.

- Exceptional working capital management sustained sufficient headroom to keep us trading.

Bear points

- Vendor vacuum. Leigh Webb was a strong character who understood his business and market extremely well. He was also a *tour de force* managerially, driving his team hard. The operations director who was anointed managing director couldn't fill the gap.

- Poultry is a natural product and accordingly is an unpredictable business. In the good times it prints money. When nature decides the market is to swing (e.g. inclement weather reduces the supply of grain, so the price of feed rockets - thus reducing profits of poultry producers significantly), the drivers are beyond the control of any management team, who are left to grapple with the consequences.

- A combination of cost increases and market price reduction for poultry (the latter purely caused by global factors) meant the profit levels in the business plan were never going to be achieved. My own back-of-fag-packet scratchings convinced me of this within weeks of taking the chair. At an introductory lunch with the Barclays acquisition finance manager, I broke the news to him that as far as I could see profit was going to be half the plan levels.

- 3i and the banks were initially shocked by the revised projections, and we had to swing into full *work-out* mode.

Success or failure

With the benefit of hindsight, the rescue of Webb's was an extraordinary achievement by its very hard-pressed management. From a hopeless situation, sheer hard work and some ingenuity led to the company not only avoiding receivership, but actually going on to repay all senior debt and achieve a substantial recovery in equity value.

The exit

The board realised that without fundamental improvement in the industry's supply and demand balance, more favourable market conditions would remain illusory. Industry consolidation was necessary as costs would need to be reduced even further and the synergies of mergers were required to achieve this. The arguments were strong and in all major poultry players' interests.

The band struck up and the *musical chairs* of industry consolidation got under way. Finally another UK player, Faccenda, saw the logic and acquired Webb's as a going concern for cash. Peter Walton and the executive team did an outstanding job in convincing them of the attraction of merging both companies. His job done, Peter Walton departed.

This left the business with three assets: Brian Watkins, myself and a freehold waterfront site with a derelict chicken factory on it at Lymington in Hampshire, valued in the books at £1.2m.

We convinced the banks not to go for immediate winding up, but to put us in funds to allow proper marketing of the site to potential buyers. They agreed and two years later, after countless meetings with planners, councillors, residents groups, politicians, developers etc. we accepted a bid from an Israeli developer, with a penchant for waterfront sites, for £10.5m.

Piers Coleman, a partner in the real estate practice of Kirkpatrick & Lockhart Nicholson Graham, succeeded as part of the sale process with a VAT registration which enabled us to reclaim a considerable sum worth a multiple of his fees. A great example of a high quality lawyer adding real value to a deal.

The banks were repaid in full, and 3i achieved a very significant write-back on their investment.

Epilogue

Faccenda merged the operations of the two companies and has traded well since. A combination of significant cost savings and an improvement in market conditions has allowed the enlarged business to prosper.

The waterfront site at Lymington is being developed as a mixed use site and will, when finished, improve the attractiveness of the town's water frontage substantially.

Figure 9.5: MBO/MBI scorecard for Webb's Country Foods Ltd

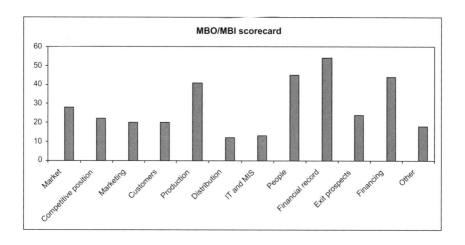

Cloverleaf Group Ltd

The opportunity to exit from the MBO in 1991 was missed and successive acquisitions went awry. Trading deteriorated necessitating a full work-out scenario. Interim management bolstered the executive team and two trade sales restored equity to value.

Background and milestones

The company was formed in London, in 1942, making cork gaskets for the war effort. After the war some entrepreneurial fellow had the idea of decorating the middle-bits, which were punched out, and selling them as table mats.

The business relocated to Swindon in 1956 with a 25-year lease on a property on the Cheney Manor industrial estate. It was purchased by the Finegold brothers in 1966, and rapidly expanded, reaching turnover of roughly £10m by 1979, working from five separate production sites. It subsequently relocated to a single site. This site, leased at a very attractive rate (from the landlord's perspective), ultimately became a millstone around the company's neck.

The business began Far East sourcing in early 1980s – one of the early-movers in the industry to do so. The Finegold family sold the business to the Tootal Group plc in 1986 for approximately £7m.

In 1987, Tootal decided to expand the company by acquisition, and bought TG Green, a ceramics and pottery business, adding a second site to the reforming group.

In turn, Tootal was acquired by Coats Viyella in 1991. The acquirer decided Cloverleaf was non-core, and sold it to management for £4.1m.

Performance for the first two years was very satisfactory, with growth in turnover and profitability. However, the company then set out on what proved to be a series of ill-fated acquisitions: Woodhaven Products of Christchurch in 1993, added bathroom cabinets; Pearson Pottery of Chesterfield in 1994, brought more pottery; and finally, KJ Bushill Ltd of Watford in 1995, yet more cabinets.

The plan was to achieve growth, but the bloated business ended up with higher overheads and wafer-thin margin on the new acquisitions. The unfocused group lost momentum and turnover, and profit began to fall.

The original managing director was replaced by the finance director, Paul Callaghan, in 1998 and the only non-executive director on the board retired. I was invited by NatWest Equity Partners to join the board and assist management in improving performance and thereafter to identify, and achieve, an exit.

Backers

- Equity: NatWest Equity Partners and management (35:65).

- Debt: Bank of Scotland and Banc Boston.

Highlights and lessons

Timing of the MBO's exit – *carpe diem*!

Cloverleaf missed the boat. This MBO completed in 1991 and could have exited with a trade sale three years later. It didn't, because the board apparently couldn't agree. I joined the board in 1998, and by then poor performance meant survival, rather than exit, dominated the board's agenda.

Needless to say, performance had been patchy over the seven-year period since the MBO.

Paul Callaghan freely admitted how the board had blown it by failing to go for the exit earlier. Instead, the company had endured some eye-poppingly bad trading, as the heat of competition from the Far East was increasingly felt in the UK home wares industry.

By 1998 the company was haemorrhaging cash, profit and customers.

Salami-slicing the forecast means you are in denial

Throughout 1998, trading continued to deteriorate. It was a classic case of management being in denial. I told board colleagues this forcefully on several occasions and could see the look on their faces, which suggested that it was me who had lost the plot. The business was in the early stages of a tail-spin, and at almost every board meeting the year-end forecast was salami-sliced again. The bank could see the problem and, predictably, the account with HBOS was moved from Bristol into the tender loving care of Credit Lending Services at Reading.

Management had enjoyed a good, long-term relationship with the BOS team in Bristol. The transfer to Reading actually helped, in that management had to accept reality and face the challenges this would represent.

Preserving the lifeblood – cash management

The BOS team in Reading quickly got to grips with their new patient and, while reassuring management of their desire to help the company turn the corner, they also set about reducing their exposure and risk.

This saw them deploy a *cash-sweep*, which hoovered any spare cash out of the business, and set up an *invoice discounting* facility. Cash is a company's lifeblood, and it is the one resource which is desperately needed in a situation like this. The setting of a non-negotiable limit on the facilities was the icing on the cake. The company now had very limited room for manoeuvre. It was the classic Catch-22 situation: to become profitable the company had to reduce costs; to reduce costs it had to lose people; and to lose people meant incurring costs; and costs equals cash. So, to survive we needed cash – the one thing we were fast running out of.

Paul and Malcolm Howell (the very capable financial controller) were taking the brunt of the strain. On the one hand, they were trying to run a business and all that that entails, on the other, they were wrestling with producing more forecasts and projections for the bank, and explaining any significant discrepancies. We were the hamsters on the treadmill: running ever faster, but getting truly nowhere.

The value of a work-out professional

We needed a fresh perspective and a fresh pair of legs. They arrived in the form of Bryan Thomson – a work-out professional.

It was plain to me that, without help, management were going to be overrun by the increasing demands. One difficulty was how to persuade Paul

Callaghan to accept that this was genuine help, and not a plot to introduce his successor. He was perfectly entitled to be suspicious, as banks in particular don't hesitate to change board members if they consider it necessary. I persuaded Paul that the right role for Bryan was as deputy managing director. Bryan was blessed with good people skills, alongside his ability to find cost savings and generate cash out of seemingly nothing.

He also fitted in well, forming an effective and tight unit with Paul and Malcolm Howell. They handled the bank and its work-out team (reporting accountants) very well. The latter arrived to advise the bank of their risk and options.

I have no doubt that, without the addition of Bryan to the team, the company would have lost the confidence of the bank and would have subsequently gone into administration. Paul and Malcolm, no matter how hard they had worked, simply would have been overwhelmed by the demands being made on them.

Finding a way out

Paul Callaghan made some tough but vital changes to his management team. As part of the plan to cut costs, he had streamlined the board, and we were finally becoming a more effective team. Cherry Jones managed the M&S account increasingly well, while Jeremy Redshaw played a blinder in managing both production sites (as well as an expanding young family).

After months of reducing SKUs (the number of product lines), improved design and packaging, revised shift patterns, better terms with suppliers and outsourcing non-core activities, we were slowly increasing margins and customer service levels. Some cash was beginning to be generated. However the body blows were still landing: the M&S drive to increase their margins affected us, a delisting with Tesco and a host of other setbacks would periodically test our resolve.

I was at a Tubex board in Aberaman and received a message from Bryan Thompson. His level of concern was rising; we simply weren't making enough progress quickly enough. He felt we should meet that evening in Swindon. I arrived to find both him and Paul Callaghan in uncharacteristically downbeat mode. We joked a little and lightened the mood (by discussing football: Paul, a long-suffering Notts Forest man; Bryan, a Sunderland fan; while Malcolm and I were Swindon Town supporters).

As Swindon Town fans, with only one significant trophy in decades, we had the ultimate training in how to treat each setback as an impostor. We sat and talked through the need to achieve more. The more we talked, the more it dawned upon us that we simply had to close the Church Gresley manufacturing site. No matter what the difficulties were, we just had to get it done. We got on the front foot, and began to think through how we could do the impossible: close this old site, meet the redundancy costs, and relocate vital elements of production to Swindon – without spending a penny.

Lessons

- Dysfunctional management teams have a marked effect on a business. The original MBO team was riven with various conflicts, which were cruelly exposed as the business began to experience significant difficulties. Several of the principals left one at a time between 1997 and 2001.

- The venture capitalist, sitting on a minority stake, has little power to influence board decisions and strategy.

Board matters

- From 1998, Paul Callaghan was combined chairman and CEO of the business and I was the solitary non-executive director.

- Financial information was excellent. However, lack of investment in a broader management information system meant the business struggled to get to grips with working capital, in particular stock and production.

- The rump of the board became more cohesive, as, one by one, members of the original MBO peeled away.

- Paul Callaghan fostered a great team spirit and loyalty from his remaining colleagues. The business would have failed without the dedication and resourcefulness of the core team which remained.

- The board was strengthened by the addition of professional turnaround management – Bryan Thompson made a substantial contribution. It was to Paul Callaghan's credit that he allowed him to get fully involved as he devolved real decision-making power.

Strategy

The business was a fully integrated manufacturer and marketer of various household goods and home wares to UK major multiples (e.g. M&S, Debenhams, House of Fraser and Tesco).

It had to reinvent itself as a designer, procurer and marketer of its product portfolio, and progressively reduce the proportion of goods produced in its own plants.

Performance

Bull points

- **Overheads** were reduced significantly.

- **Customer service** levels were improved as the business ruthlessly reduced the number of lines produced.

- The **slimmed down board** became focused and effective.

- The **management team** were mutually supportive.

- **Professional turnaround management resources** were introduced to augment the management team.

- The TG Green **plant in the potteries was sold** as a going concern, freeing up cash and reducing costs.

- **Working capital and cash management** improved dramatically.

- A **trade buyer** was identified.

- **Backers were demanding but supportive.** Their patience enabled a solution to be found.

Bear points

- The original MBO achieved some success, but then **lost its way** with a series of acquisitions which failed.

- **Successive acquisition strategies are difficult.** To succeed requires a very clear sense of direction and strong management to achieve the necessary cost savings and synergies – especially when debt needs to be serviced and repaid.

- Many of the **company's products could be manufactured in the Far East** and delivered to the UK, at substantially lower prices than could be achieved by producing locally. One memorable episode saw the proofed-up samples of some tableware, requested by management while at a trade show in Hong Kong, arrive back at Swindon before the management team!

- **Marks & Spencer was an important customer.** They began to increasingly use go-betweens to source their requirements at better margins from overseas.

- **Time taken to recover and turn around** performance took longer than expected.

- **Lack of long-term investment in IT and systems** hindered management and decision-making.

- **Long-term inflexible leasehold commitments** were expensive and a millstone.

- **Intense competition** reduced gross margin.

Success or failure

- First exit opportunity missed which unquestionably cost the MBO team dearly.

- Woeful financial performance drove the business to the verge of insolvency.

- The work-out situation was a success:

  - avoided receivership;

  - recovered all the bank debt for HBOS;

  - the defined benefits pension scheme was closed, and in so doing the rights of members were protected and preserved; and

  - partially restored equity value for Bridgepoint and management.

The exit

What happened

The slimmed down Cloverleaf was sold to Pimpernel Ltd, which had recently been bought by its own management, backed by 3i. Their strategy was to buy-and-build a home wares group based in the UK.

Results for stakeholders

Some value was restored for equity, so management and NatWest Equity Partners (by then Bridgepoint Capital) were delighted. HBOS were paid out completely.

Epilogue

Most of the senior management at Cloverleaf departed at the takeover or shortly thereafter. The market remains very competitive, and it is said that more UK customers are sourcing direct from either via disintermediators or direct from overseas manufacturers.

No doubt the management team and backers at Pimpernel will be considering their own exit plans at some stage.

Figure 9.6: MBO/MBI scorecard for Cloverleaf Group Ltd

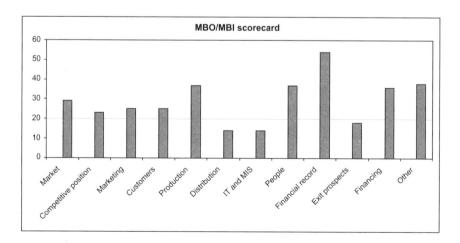

Ashford Colour Press Ltd

A highly successful entrepreneur sells his company to the management team he developed. After a rocky start the team flourish and the business achieves strong growth.

Background and milestones

Ashford Colour Press was formed in 1980 as a partnership by the then owners, bringing together two print farming businesses and introducing manufacturing. Led by Mr Norman Betts, a naturally gifted entrepreneur, the business grew substantially on the back of investing in new printing technologies. In the late 1980s and early 1990s it moved away from general commercial colour printing into niche markets, mainly educational books. It has since moved into the legal and professional manual market and, more recently, the software games book market. In 1999, the partnership was incorporated and the following year it moved to its current 45,000 sq foot site in Gosport.

The founder built the business by providing excellent customer service to substantial, nationwide customers. The service was under-pinned by heavy investment in capital goods, which achieved high levels of efficiency, price competitiveness and quality in the finished product.

Norman Betts had developed his management into a formidable team, and was keen to sell the business to them as he wished to see them continue what he had started. He is a very keen windsurfer and sailor and set his sights on early retirement, enjoying his hobbies.

Beringea appointed their own non-executive director; I was introduced to the team and became chairman after completion.

Backers

*   Equity was provided by Beringea Ltd.
*   Debt finance was courtesy of the Royal Bank of Scotland.

Highlights and lessons

1. *A deal which works for both sides can be achieved without an auction.*
   The deal was completed in 2001, at a price which met the vendor's aspiration – enabling him to pursue a very active retirement in the Caribbean.

2. *Plugging a gap.*
   The FD's position was a new one, as before the MBO finance functions were supplied by another company the vendor was involved with. This had to be filled after completion and a plan existed to achieve this.

3. *A high quality management team.*
   The management team are extremely capable as individuals, but are at their best as a unit. While they argue strongly about various issues, they never quarrel. Their support and respect for each other is a great attribute. (This is doubly surprising as the team contains Southampton and Pompey fans!)

4. *Man overboard.*
   The new finance director didn't work out. After three months the business was still flying blind, and the personal chemistry between him and the executive directors was poor. An interim finance director was brought in and carried out the necessary tasks, while we searched and found the right candidate.

5. *High levels of investment can continue in an MBO.*
   The company's business model has always relied upon high levels of capital investment to achieve high levels of quality and efficiency and to keep costs competitive. Further, sales have grown by around 20% since the deal was completed, and so additional capacity was required. The financing structure put in place has allowed further financing to continue.

Board matters

Composition

Beringea appointed Stuart Veale as their non-executive director. Following his promotion, to run their UK operation, he handed over to Jeff Bocan. Andy Hulse, the financial controller, attends all meetings.

Good board/bad board

- Excellent management information.

- Good rapport and open debate.

- Key issues well-covered.

- Meetings usually 2-3 hours.

- Separate strategy meeting.

Strategy

The strategy was more of the same for the MBO – growth from additional sales with existing customers, supplemented by the development of a small number of new accounts. The focus on the premium sectors of the market remained, and investment in capital to achieve high levels of efficiency and cost-effectiveness continued.

Performance

Bull points

- The team settled down quickly and sales growth continued.

- Initial problems with the new finance director and the management information system were addressed quickly and decisively.

- An experienced and very capable interim finance director, Tony Grimstone, supplemented by Hurst, Morris and Thompson (a firm of accountants who offer this specialised support), identified the problems and what was needed to resolve them.

- A new financial controller, Andy Hulse, was recruited. He gelled straight away and has implemented the solutions to the management information system.

- The deal was well-structured. It proved flexible and able to cope comfortably with the continuing programme of capital investment and the initial teething problems.

- Communications improved as management have invested in new technology.

Bear points

- The new finance director failed to achieve vital objectives. He didn't gel with the team or implement the systems necessary to produce the management accounts. After three months we were still flying blind, and backers were alarmed and restless.

- The original business plan proved over-optimistic in the first year. The figures were recast within six months of completion, and all financial targets have been met since.

The exit

- The company is backed by venture capital funds which are able to take a longer-term view of the investment.

- Strong cash performance has enabled debt to be repaid ahead of plan.

- If performance remains above plan, the management will have options; one of which would be to refinance and acquire Beringea's equity with a secondary MBO.

Epilogue

The company is approaching its third year as an MBO and performing ahead of the current plan. New customers have been won and sales have increased significantly. The capital investment programme continues to increase capacity and improve efficiencies and customer service.

Figure 9.7: MBO/MBI scorecard for Ashford Colour Press Ltd

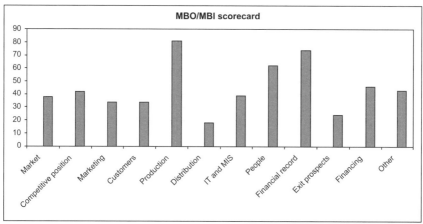

Dennis-Eagle Ltd

A divided board detached from divisional management, and too high a price paid, almost ends in disaster. Swift work-out action and high quality support from the venture capitalist saves the day, and a secondary MBO is achieved.

My role was as executive coach to the managing director of Dennis-Eagle Ltd, Mike Molesworth. I was not exposed directly to the workings of the business – he and I would meet monthly and communicate as needed in-between on various issues as they arose. The hard work was entirely from Mike and his team; they achieved a truly impressive turnaround in their fortunes. I'm very grateful to him for his help in compiling this section on his company.

Background and milestones

Dennis-Eagle Ltd bashes heavy metal. They make dustcarts and are based in the heart of the West Midlands. Dennis-Eagle Ltd was part of Dennis Group, which was acquired by the now infamous Mayflower in December 1998.

Mayflower put the business up for sale through an auction, and bundled in two other small businesses to create a mini-group of three companies – Dennis-Eagle Ltd was the juiciest morsel.

Backers

- **Equity**: NatWest Equity Partners (now Bridgepoint Capital) won the auction for £32m in July 1999. The figure was to prove too high.

- **Debt**: Société Generale provided the debt and syndicated 50% to Royal Bank of Scotland.

Highlights and lessons

These are less descriptive than in the other deals covered as I was involved as a coach to the managing director rather than privy to the board meetings and detailed workings of the business.

1. Dennis-Eagle's previous highest EBIT was £3m.

2. The two other businesses combined were only marginally profitable: this was very cyclical and dependant on a small number of customers.

3. A group was created called VSNV in Belgium to acquire the target companies.

4. All existing management were retained, yet not incentivised with sweet equity.

5. The Dennis-Eagle management had minimal input into the plan.

6. Group management consisted of a non-executive chairman and group financial director.

7. Management consultants were used to identify profit improvement opportunities – the benefits of which were included the financial projections.

Board matters

- The MDs of the three operating companies attended the group's board meetings, and the group's chairman and finance director attended the Dennis-Eagle Ltd board meetings.

- The non-executive chairman represented one of the institutional shareholders and, as such, was not able to be fully independent.

- Management saw the group board as a conduit for reporting back to the shareholders. It apparently did not discuss strategy or focus upon the key issues in the operating businesses.

- The situation, described by Mike Molesworth the managing director of Dennis-Eagle Ltd, "became unsatisfactory when decisions were necessary concerning additional funding".

- The board was later significantly strengthened through Bridgepoint's support and intervention. The group FD left and an independent chairman was appointed.

Strategy

The strategy of the original MBO appeared to be financially driven - a bundling exercise, with some cost savings, which would exit via a trade sale having achieved an uplift in value.

Performance

Bull points

- Initially the performance of the two smaller businesses was ahead of expectations; however, they were heavily dependent on business from the major airlines. They were both severely affected in the aftermath of September 11th.

- In the wake of the short-term crisis, realistic expectations supplanted the original rose-tinted optimism.

- Dennis-Eagle Ltd management prepared, and thus felt accountable for, the revised business plan and were incentivised to achieve it.

- The *group* board was disbanded and management changes were made at group level. The group finance director departed and the non-executive chairman was replaced.

- The shareholder's ability and preparedness to understand the core problems, belief in the businesses potential and willingness to provide new money quickly averted a potentially serious situation.

- Revised business sales and profit targets were met.

Bear points

- The original board proved not to be effective in managing the business in difficult situations.

- Divisional management did not own the original business plan which they inherited.

- The business was hit by a double whammy of a severe downturn in orders coupled to several key suppliers going bust (which delayed the fulfilment of orders). The effect of this precipitated a short-term cash crunch and banking covenants were broken. Dennis-Eagle Ltd was in the dreaded work-out territory.

- The price paid for the business proved to be too high. The cost savings were unrealistic.

- The strategy unravelled in its execution. Instead of disposing of the two out-riding-divisions, they were maintained. This resulted in less focus on Dennis-Eagle.

The exit

- Bridgepoint reverted to the original plan, which was to dispose of the non-core businesses as soon as possible and review Dennis-Eagle when the first stages of the plan were completed.

- In the event, Dennis-Eagle exceeded expectations in the second year. Bridgepoint decided to seek an immediate exit, since it was clear that the next stage of transformation would take about three years and probably result in further acquisitions.

- Secondary MBO completed in January 2004 for £51m. This, coupled with the proceeds of the sale of the other two businesses and allowing for the additional debt to finance the acquisition, resulted in an equity gain of just less than £10m, and the repayment of all shareholder loans and accrued interest.

- Whilst the institutional shareholders did not meet their target returns, they nevertheless made a reasonable gain on the disposal of a group for which they paid too much originally, and had missed its covenants necessitating a re-financing after three-years.

- Management were able to take out some of their gain, but largely reinvested in the secondary MBO and achieved a larger equity stake.

Epilogue

The business is now owned by:

- ABN Amro Capital, 49%;
- Lloyds Development Capital, 31%;
- Management, 20%.

£25m of senior debt is provided by Royal Bank of Scotland (the original backers with Société Générale) who have syndicated a part to Bank of Ireland.

The board includes all investee managers and has an independent chairman. Board meetings concentrate on strategic issues whilst ensuring proper oversight of the operations.

At the end of 2004, a year after the secondary buy-out, Dennis-Eagle achieved their first year profit and cash targets, setting records for financial, sales and production performance. The cash position at the end of the year will enable the business to pay down senior debt, ahead of schedule, by £1.5m.

Figure 9.8: MBO/MBI scorecard for Dennis-Eagle Ltd

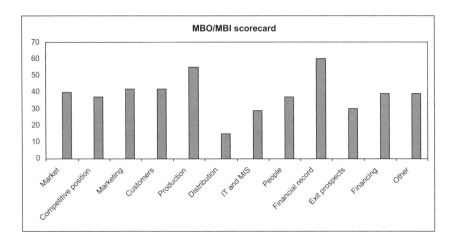

Chapter 10

The Exit

Desires of management

These are obviously vital in determining the type and timing of any exit, not least because the management team might be, at least in part, what an acquirer may be buying. This is often the case in a trade sale. In a flotation, the investors are tangibly backing management and will require comfort that the individuals will stay the course.

The venture capitalist knows the importance of solidarity between MBO/MBI principals on an exit, and may well seek to gain broad agreement on principles before completion of the original MBO/MBI.

However, circumstances change over time, and things become complicated when there is a divergence between MBO/MBI principals on what they are ultimately trying to achieve from an exit. If these have arisen, the non-executive directors and the venture capitalist have a key role in brokering an agreement between the parties.

Management: realising cash from the exit

Trade sale

When management depart amicably, perhaps as part of a trade sale, they can ordinarily realise value from their equity straight away.

If the management team intend staying on with the business after the exit, the amount they are able to cash-in from their equity becomes another hurdle to be overcome. This will vary by the type of exit, but, generally, new investors are sympathetic to some cash being realised by the original MBO/MBI investors; however, if too much of management's stake is cashed-in, the issue of the future incentivisation of the management team rears its ugly head. Any investor wants to see the interests of the management team aligned with their own. A compromise is usually achieved but often only after some quite difficult debate.

Flotation

In the case of flotations, institutional investors have learnt to be very wary of directors' share sales, having been burnt by many high profile cases in the past. It is regretfully the case that several directors have sold stock indecently close to the subsequent emergence of bad news – which hits their company's share price. Some investment publications and websites watch directors' dealings like a hawk, and use it as the basis upon which to form investment decisions in companies.

Investor needs and expectations

Venture capitalists need exits to crystallise value in their funds. They will have raised their fund(s) from investors with a promise of a return on that capital with which they have been entrusted. No exit, no return.

A venture capitalist's return is the composite of their success and failure with investments in MBOs/MBIs. They are in the risk/reward business.

The investment return they achieve is principally driven by:

1. The proportion of their investments:

    - which achieve a significant uplift in value on exit;

    - which stagnates and goes sideways for years; and

    - which goes bust.

2. How quickly can they crystallise value from exits? The internal rate of return (IRR) is a key driver of the performance of their fund. A key determinant of the IRR is time, thus there is always an attraction to take the money early.*

3. The running yield they earn on equity (preference shares pay interest).

4. The repayment of chunks of redeemable equity.

---

* An exception to this is venture capital trusts. These succeeded the old Business Enterprise Schemes (BES) and were established by legislation in 1995. These are often managed by venture capitalists, are invested in unquoted businesses and offer their own investors significant tax advantages. Because they are designed to run for seven years before closing, their managers can usually take a longer-term view on exit.

Importance of timing

If performance of the MBO/MBI has been on or above plan you will be in control of the timing of the exit. However, there is no one-size-fits-all solution. The timing decision is an amalgam of judgements, personal desires, competitive actions, approaches, needs, circumstances, greed, market sentiment, and a host of other issues; many of which you will recognise as being beyond your control.

> Timing the exit is so multi-faceted it is often a mistake to try to over-finesse this.

Unforeseen circumstances and events are also likely to be a driver. The range of factors which can affect an exit can be used by management teams and boards to prevaricate endlessly. Narcissus was the figure in Greek mythology that spent so long gazing at his reflection in a pool that he went into a trance, toppled in, and drowned. There is a lesson here!

The best advice is: if a genuine opportunity presents itself, look at it seriously and if it is doable, with an acceptable return, go for it. *Carpe diem.*

Prerequisites

These obviously vary by the type of exit preferred and are covered later in this chapter. The key items below are essential prerequisites to any exit and need to be considered carefully.

1. The likely uplift in value, based on the price the exit is forecasted to achieve, is **acceptable to the equity investors** (implicit here is that the business has a record of financial results over at least a three-year period which support the price being sought).

2. The **business will bear the scrutiny of due diligence.** There is little point setting out on a process if a black hole torpedoes value or scuppers the entire process (witness recent pensions black holes doing just this).

3. **Consensus amongst the management team** that the exit route is the right one. If one half of the team wants retirement, and the other half a secondary MBO, there is a problem.

4.   There are **no identifiable major threats** just over the horizon which are going to adversely affect the business's present trajectory (e.g. potential changes in a tax or duty regime by the Chancellor of the Exchequer).

5.   That the **chosen exit is realistic** (e.g. there is no point floating in a major recession, or trying to sell to a trade buyer who, unbeknown to you, is breaching its banking covenants).

Exit timing – what is realistic?

Chart 10.1: Exit percentage of buy-outs by vintage year and value range

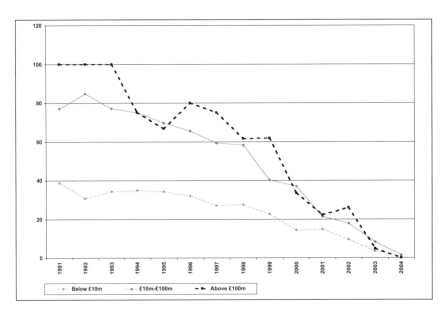

Source: CMBOR/Barclays Private Equity/Deloitte

Although most venture capitalists aim for an exit in 3-5 years, evidence shows that this is not always achieved. In the early 1990s the average time taken to exit was three and a half years; by 2001 this had risen to over five years. There is also a marked difference in the timing achieved in relation to the size of the original MBO/MBI. Perhaps, understandably, the larger the deal, the quicker the exit.

MBOs/MBIs over £100m have the best track record, with almost three quarters of such investments made in 1997 now realised. Conversely, only a quarter of the sub £10m deals made in the same year have achieved this.

CMBOR estimate the total value of unrealised equity in venture capitalists' UK portfolios at £37bn. However, it's believed that in many of these cases the venture capitalist has a minority equity position, and thus no effective control over the exit.

Exit value

Chart 10.2: Exit numbers and exit values, 1995-2004

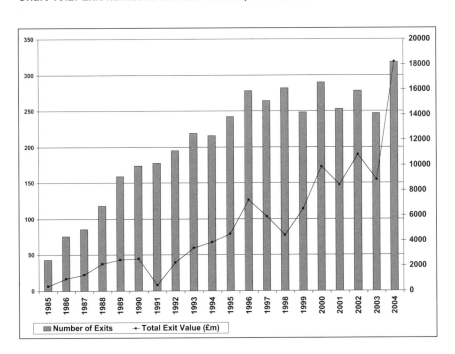

Source: CMBOR/Barclays Private Equity/Deloitte

The chart shows a general growth trend both in the number and value of exits. It's notable that the total value of exit values in 2004 was more than double the previous year.

Types of exit

See chart 7.1 (UK buy-outs/buy-ins by type of exit) on page 85 for a comparison of exit types.

The main options for exit are: receivership (which has accounted for almost a third of all exits); trade sale; secondary MBOs/MBIs; or flotation. These are examined in more detail below.

The most notable trends are the decline in flotations, which has fuelled the growth in secondary MBOs/MBIs; while the fact that receivership is the most common exit is a somewhat sobering fact.

Table 10.1: Major exits in 2004 (non-floats)

Transaction	Value of deal (£m)	Value on exit (£m)	Year of exit	Purchaser deal
Unique Pub & Voyager Pub/ The Pub Estate/Unique Pub Company	2,013.0	2,300.0	2002	Enterprise Inns
Saga Group	54.3	1,350.0	1990	Secondary buy-out
CrestaCare/Four Seasons Healthcare	70.4	775.0	1999	Secondary buy-out
Savoy Group	520.0	750.0	1998	Quinlan Private
Newmond Ltd/Baxi Group Ltd	360.0	663.0	1996	Secondary buy-out
Westminster Health Care	267.0	525.0	2002	Barchester Healthcare
BTR Aerospace/Dunlop Standard Aerospace	510.0	408.4	1998	Meggitt plc
Imo Carwash Group	138.0	350.0	1998	Secondary buy-out
Ushers of Trowbridge/InnSpired	107.8	335.0	1999	Punch Taverns
Safety-Kleen	126.6	274.0	1998	Secondary buy-out
Premium Credit/Vendcrown	40.3	250.0	1996	MBNA Europe Bank/Corp (USA)
Earls Court & Olympia Group	183.0	245.0	1999	St James Capital (Property Co)
Maplin	42.0	244.0	2001	Secondary buy-out
Commodore Group	150.0	240.0	2002	Secondary buy-out
Alcontrol Laboratories	72.2	240.0	2000	Secondary buy-out
Paramount Hotels	77.0	215.0	1998	Secondary buy-out
Haefely Trench/Trench Electric Holdings	164.0	190.0	1997	Siemens
Oxoid Holdings/Oxoid 2000	112.0	177.5	2000	Fisher Scientific Inter Inc
Bourne Leisure/Park Resorts	45.5	165.0	2001	Secondary buy-out
Southern Cross Healthcare (SCH)	80.0	162.0	2002	Secondary buy-out
Whitbread Pubs/Laurel Pub Company	1,630.0	151.0	2001	R20 - Last disposal 160 bars
Wardle Storeys/Edlaw/Air-Sea Survival Equipment (ASSE)	113.6	146.0	2000	Secondary buy-out
Dualwise Ltd	12.0	135.0	1990	Secondary buy-out
Western Wines	53.0	135.0	2002	Vincor International (Canada)
Edotech	14.3	130.0	2000	Astron UK00001
Morris Homes	35.0	127.0	1998	Secondary buy-out
Ethel Austin	55.0	122.5	2002	Secondary buy-out
HPI	70.0	120.0	2003	Norwich Union plc subsiduary
Hillarys Blinds/Hillarys Group	50.0	115.0	2001	Secondary buy-out
Hobbs	30.0	111.0	2002	Secondary buy-out
Goldsmiths/Mildghosts Limited	77.1	110.0	1999	Baugur (Iceland)
Leisure Great Britain/GB Holiday Parks	40.0	105.0	2001	Secondary buy-out
Transaction Technology/IRIS Software	32.0	102.0	2000	Secondary buy-out
Jimmy Choo/Equinox Luxury Holdings	10.6	101.0	2001	Secondary buy-out
Cabot Financial Europe	n.d.	100.0	1999	Secondary buy-out
Galileo Brick	90.0	98.9	2002	Wienerberger (Austria)
BPB Wireline/Reeves Oilfield Services	13.5	92.4	1995	Precision Drilling Corp (Canada)
Nightfreight (Ewenny)	49.5	89.0	2001	Secondary buy-out
Tracker Network	39.2	80.0	1999	Royal Bank of Scotland Insurance
Sherman Cooper/Ben Sherman	120.0	80.0	2000	Oxford Industries (US)
SLSS - OYEZ/Oyez Straker	25.0	80.0	1996	Secondary buy-out
1st Credit Limited	16.0	80.0	2002	Secondary buy-out
Vardon Attractions/Merlin Entertainments	50.0	72.5	1998	Secondary buy-out
HFS Group	33.5	65.0	2004	Capital one
Pharmaceuticals Limited/Penn Pharmaceutical Services	12.0	62.5	2000	Celgene Corp (USA)
Early Learning Centre Holdings	44.0	62.0	2001	Secondary buy-out
Robert Dyas	n.d.	61.0	2001	Secondary buy-out
MORI/Market & Opinion Research Int	32.0	55.0	2000	Secondary buy-out
Bowater Windows (Hamsard 2064)	n.d.	52.0	2002	Secondary buy-out
Waddington Jaycare	29.0	51.5	2000	Secondary buy-out
Vehicle Solutions (Mayflower)	31.0	51.0	1999	Secondary buy-out
MCB Press	55.0	50.0	1998	Secondary buy-out

Source: CMBOR/Barclays Private Equity/Deloitte

Trade sale

A *trade sale* is the disposal of a company's shares or assets (and liabilities), in whole or in part, to another company. The purchasing company may be a *strategic buyer*, who intends to grow his business, or a *financial buyer*, who wants to generate a financial return on his invested capital at the time of exit.

A trade sale is usually the best way to get a good financial exit from a small firm, particularly if you have several competing buyers.

Trade buyers are often welcome as they know a lot about your company and your market. They can also often afford to pay a *strategic premium*. This arises when your business or brand may be one of only a few likely to be available in the foreseeable future.

Trade buyers can also usually achieve synergies. Although, as mentioned before, Lord Hanson described synergies as being like yetis "Everyone talks about them, but no one has ever seen one", the fact remains, that a trade buyer can potentially afford to pay a rich price, this is because:

- they can reduce costs by eliminating duplicated overheads;

- the addition of your business to theirs may provide them with competitive advantages based on scale economies or brand clout; and

- because of their knowledge, the amount of due diligence they may need to carry out is relatively modest.

Identify possible buyers of your business

- You are more likely to know them than any advisor as they probably work in your market.

- Corporate advisors can assist with databases and other contacts, possibly international ones.

- Try and identify the strategic buyers (i.e. those who can afford to pay a premium for your business, either because they can make cost savings by eliminating replicated costs or by taking your brands or services into new markets).

- Trade magazines and exhibitions can be a useful way of identifying buyers.

- A contested auction nearly always achieves a higher price.

Work to develop characteristics buyers look for

- Access to new markets or customers: yours or theirs.

- Industry consolidation.

- Access to a particular brand or service which increases their market share.

- Management or staff which deliver skills they need.

- Cost savings – highlighting those which are relatively easy to achieve (i.e. 'low-hanging fruit').

Secondary MBO/MBI

These have become more popular in recent years. Very simply, another VC sees advantages or a value play in acquiring your company. It may be part of a *buy-and-build*, where he seeks to combine you with a company they presently own, or they simply have the hots for your sector.

The process is much the same as the original one except, of course, management teams can find themselves facing both ways at once. They will be required to sell the business effectively to themselves, with the quest for value on the exit perhaps tempered by living with the consequences of over-paying.

Flotation

Chart 10.3: Buy-outs as percentage of all London Stock Exchange Flotations

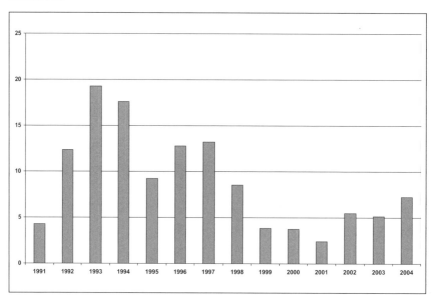

Source: CMBOR/Barclays Private Equity/Deloitte

Table 10.2: Buy-out/buy-in flotations in 2004

Transaction	Value of deal (£m)	Value on exit (£m)	Year of deal	Year of float	Month of float
Supply Desk/Project Socrates/ Public Recruitment Group	12.0	30.0	2002	2004	April.
British Biocell International (BBI)	4.8	10.0	2000	2004	April.
Dignity Caring Funeral Services/ Dignity Services	220.0	184.0	2002	2004	April.
PKL Holdings	8.5	40.0	1995	2004	April.
Software Dialog & Panda/Formjet	2 (Est)	4.7	2003	2004	August.
Immunodiagnostic Systems	1.5	7.4	1996	2004	December.
Ratheon Marine/Raymarine	74.0	125.5	2001	2004	December.
Staffline	5.7	16.7	2000	2004	December.
GOALS (Glasgow Open Air Leisure)/ Fortis Leisure	16.0	26.0	2000	2004	December.
ArmorGroup/Armor Products International	20.0	31.0	2003	2004	December.
Rebus	190.0	152.9	1999	2004	January.
Hillsdown/Premier Foods	822.0	527.0	1999	2004	July.
Prologic Computer Consultants	3.9	6.5	1999	2004	July.
Marconi Applied Technology/ technologies Ltd	57.0	86.7	2002	2004	July.e2v
NCC Group	30.0	65.0	2003	2004	July.
MKM Marketing & Promotions	0.8	5.8	2002	2004	June.
Halfords	427.0	593.0	2002	2004	June.
Umbro	90.0	144.5	1999	2004	June.
ATH Resources	2 (Est)	40.2	1998	2004	June.
Banner Business Supplies/ O2O/office2office	10.0	64.6	2001	2004	June.
Xyratex	110 (Est)	213.0	2003	2004	June.
Torex retail business/Lynxangel	66.9	22.5	2004	2004	March.
Pinewood Studios	62.0	82.5	2000	2004	May
Star Energy/Soco	7.6	79.0	1999	2004	May.
Phoenix Computers/ Phoenix IT Group	6.5	133.0	1997	2004	November.
Bencard Allergy Business/ Allergy Therapeutics	20.0	16.0	1998	2004	October.
SmartFocus	2 (Est)	16.0	2000	2004	October.
Jessops Limited	116.0	159.0	2002	2004	October.
Freedom Group/Spice Holdings	n.d.	48.5	1996	2004	September.
Admiral Insurance Services	110.0	711.0	1999	2004	September.

Source: CMBOR/Barclays Private Equity/Deloitte

This, potentially, offers the highest price and liquidity, and is usually a golden exit. Many MBOs and MBIs have exited via flotation achieving 40-60 times multiple on the sweet equity. Unfortunately, it is increasingly difficult to achieve, because of diminishing demand for new entrants capitalised at less than £500m. Since the late 1990s the number of companies listed on London Stock Exchange has reduced substantially.

However, for companies achieving consistent high growth, or who have a justified appetite for capital, it still makes sense.

The process is, not surprisingly, quite an arduous one. In terms of effort and work load, it approaches that required to achieve an MBO/MBI.

> At Taunton Cider we achieved a flotation on the Main Market in July 1992 – fourteen months after the completion of our MBO – at over a 40 times multiplier on the sweet equity.
>
> We were fortunate to have had a five-year track record of turnover and profit growth in place, otherwise such a quick transition would be almost impossible to achieve.
>
> But, as Einstein said, "imagination is more important than knowledge". We imagined we could do it, and, supported by a formidable array of talent amongst our backers and advisors, we managed it. There were, however, very demanding issues to be dealt with. The journey was a carousel of elation and disappointment.

The present environment is demanding for companies wishing to join the Main Market or AIM

In general, institutions are still keen to have a piece of the high profile pies, where the fundamentals support the float (e.g. Virgin in 2004). Some institutions will also be driven to take part if the stock will form part of an index. Equally though, they will price to make a gain, and tough pricing negotiations are certain to be held over any company in present market conditions. The keys are still: the quality of the earnings stream; how compelling the story is; and the depth of experience of the management team.

Use of the proceeds of flotation is a key area for institutions. If the proceeds are likely to be utilised to generate earnings enhancement in the short-term (e.g. for an acquisition that may otherwise go away), and/or the management have a robust pedigree of successfully growing businesses, funds may well be forthcoming.

Most brokers currently agree that the IPO market is tight at the present time. There is a sense of a lack of quality businesses floating on the Main Market and of saturation on AIM. Introductions or very small fundraisings (sub £5m) are the staple diet on AIM.

It has been a buyers' market for some time – institutions are not giving funds or value away and are beating down multiples. Pricing to peers is at a sizeable discount (a recent float went at 12x earnings when peer comparables were trading on 18x). Consequently, intended fundraisings are being scaled back or deferred entirely. In mid-July 2004, five floats on AIM were pulled in one week, although this was probably short-term market volatility. This tends to be borne out by the increasing numbers of flotations on AIM in the latter half of 2004 when the 1,000 company barrier was breached. It is said that many companies had to reduce their price expectations.

Another indicator of pressure on institutions to make a return is that venture capitalists are now being actively encouraged to sell out 100% of their holding as institutions do not welcome an overhang in the shares. This is said to be the case even where the venture capitalist may want to retain some upside potential with a residual stake. Important told this has led to quite difficult price vs. abort discussions.

The recent phenomenon of *accelerated IPOs* has appeared – perhaps to add some zest into the market. It is also well-known that institutions have become very frustrated over seeing their assets sold to venture capitalists, only to return to the market two years later at a substantially higher price.

Halfords is such an example. It was purchased for £427m from Boots plc by an MBO backed by CVC Capital Partners in 2002, and floated less than two years later for £593m. Since then its value has climbed on the back of excellent trading results to over £700m!

To stand a chance of achieving an accelerated IPO the following criteria are required:

- market cap of approx, £150m;
- genuine auction;
- recognisable brand/product/service;
- cash generative business;
- clear and simple business strategy; and
- a strong board and management team.

In summary, flotation remains an option and can provide a cleaner and quicker exit, but the downside is most of the cards in respect of pricing are handed to the broker and its institutional clients.

London Stock Exchange – the Main Market

The London Stock Exchange's Main Market is one of the world's longest-established, best known and most liquid markets. Just under 2,000 companies, including some of the world's largest and most successful businesses, are listed on it.

Main benefits of a listing are:

1. **access to one of the world's greatest pools of capital**;

2. a well **tried and tested process**;

3. a usually **reliable and fair market value** underpinned by liquidity and a level playing field of knowledge; and

4. **enhanced profile and credibility** as a management team and business, followed and supported by a very sophisticated investment community of analysts, fund-managers and professionals.

The Main Market has excellent sector coverage from the army of analysts based in the UK's financial centres. It is attractive to institutional fund managers who are keen to invest in established companies with real potential. The Main Market has a high standard of regulation that makes it an attractive and relatively secure place for both companies and investors.

AIM

This is specifically tailored to small, growing businesses. AIM combines the benefits of a public quotation with a flexible and less demanding regulatory approach.

AIM gives companies access to the market at an earlier stage of their development, allowing them to experience the *goldfish bowl* life which awaits a public company these days. Since AIM opened in 1995, around 1,500 companies have been admitted and well in excess of £10bn has been raised collectively.

An AIM quotation provides these benefits:

*   a flexible and less demanding **regulatory regime**;

*   access to a **unique, globally respected market** and a substantial pool of capital;

- enhanced awareness and improved profile for companies;

- ability to fund acquisitions;

- a following by several respected institutions and fund-managers; and

- attractive tax benefits for private investors.

Table 10.3: Main market and AIM – summary of the main differences

	Main Market	AIM
Min. number of shares in public hands	25%	None
Trading record required	3-years	None
Shareholder approval required for substantial acquisitions and disposals	Yes	Less stringent.
Pre-vetting of admission documents	Yes	Less stringent.
Minimum market capitalisation	Yes	None
Sponsors needed for certain transactions	Yes	Yes
Nominated adviser required at all times	Yes	Yes

Advisors

The subject of selecting advisors is covered in an earlier chapter, and the same principles apply when planning your exit.

On the basis that "if it isn't broken don't fix it", many companies and management teams stick with their advisors, as trust and mutual respect will have already been forged on the initial MBO/MBI.

There are exceptions, especially in cases where specialist skill are required. For example, a major firm of accountants may have advised you through your initial deal, but if your exit plan is to sell to a trade buyer in a specific industry, then a specialised corporate boutique, of which there are many, may be a better choice.

Management's tax planning

One simple rule here: don't leave it until it's too late.

Tax avoidance is still a legitimate activity and the management team should take specialist advice before completion on this topic. Moreover, the government has introduced various incentives to encourage entrepreneurialism and the schemes are worthy of serious consideration.

Chapter 11

After the Exit?

Corporate issues

New targets to achieve

Assuming the MBO/MBI was a success, the type of exit will obviously shape the future direction of the company.

If the company floated, it will have done so on a clear strategy and a promise of financial results to its new shareholders; these will need to be delivered.

Similarly, a trade sale will also involve conformity to the plan upon which the financing is predicated. The new targets will need to be met.

The same applies to a secondary MBO/MBI.

Management – still hungry enough?

One key aspect which will have changed is that there will be some relatively wealthy management around – unless they were required to fall upon their swords as part of the deal which succeeded the MBO/MBI. Where the amounts made are life-changing, then the business is almost certainly going to be affected.

There are some serial entrepreneurs who cannot exist without living on a diet of raw meat and frequent challenges, but they are a rather special minority. For the rest of us, it can be a challenge to drag ourselves out of bed in the morning and commute to the office – especially when facing tasks which are routine, dull or downright unpleasant. When the financial reason for having to do this is removed, any normal human being is going to consider their position. Loss of momentum at the top of a company is soon noticed and often transmitted through the business.

Personal options

If you have exited successfully, there will be a number of options open to you. One is the status quo, although for the reasons covered above many people opt for change.

The table below summarises some, but by no means all, the options.

Table 11.1: Personal options

	Full-time/One organisation	Part-time/Portfolio
Salaried	Back to corporate life as an XD. Re-train and do something completely different. Switch to the public sector. Start a new company. Buy a company and run it.	Non-executive directorships. Consultancy. Interim assignments. Business angel. Switch to the public sector (NXD posts, magistrate etc).
Honorary posts	President of a society.	Professional sport e.g. chairman/treasurer of a club. Charity trustee. Patron of a society. Manage your own investments.

There are excellent career counselling services offered by specialist companies and also experienced executive coaches. It's well worth meeting them to discuss and review your goals, preferences, ambitions etc. With this level of support some personal signposts for your future will appear.

It is also a time to reflect on what you have managed to achieve. You may be able to enjoy more time with your family and find new leisure interests. As a colleague of mine used to say:

"Live every day as though it's your last – because one day it will be."

Good luck!

Chapter 12

Twelve Golden Rules for Management Teams

1. Do an MBO/MBI with your eyes wide-open

Conducting an MBO/MBI is extremely demanding. The demands on you, your colleagues, and your family and friends, will be severe: and that is just to complete the deal. After completion, the difficulties and pressures are unlikely to abate. The risks are significant – even for a well-managed and successful business. You can materially reduce the odds against you by understanding the lessons learned by those who have gone before you.

For a manager, an MBO/MBI is a life-changing experience.

2. Ensure you are an effective team

A talented group of individuals isn't enough! You must be a team. I don't need to amplify this – any senior manager will understand the difference. If there are fault-lines within management, they will be exposed.

You should make the changes considered necessary *before* you set out on the deal, or, at worst, during the deal. Afterwards is far more difficult and it might be too late.

3. Don't overpay (work to a realistic business plan)

There is an inevitable conflict between preparing a plan which, on the one hand, is achievable, and, on the other, is capable of supporting a price high enough to ensure you can buy your target company. You need to strike the right balance, which is easier said than done.

It is said that it is better to overpay for the right business, than underpay for the wrong one. The thrust of this must be right; however, if you knowingly overpay, with the purchase price predicated on optimistic numbers, you will almost certainly regret it. In any business, performance will deviate from budget or plan. In a highly-leveraged business, the margin of underperformance which can be accommodated is relatively small. Some excellent businesses have failed in this way. There was nothing wrong with the company, its management or its prospects, but its financing structure simply couldn't withstand an unforeseen financial shock to the business.

4. Choose advisors and backers you feel comfortable with

There is no shortage of accountants, legal firms, bankers and private equity houses who will have an appetite for a good deal. It is, however, important that you feel very comfortable with your advisors and backers.

Your respective commercial and career prospects will be in each others hands. There must, therefore, be openness, trust and mutual respect. This is obviously a totally personal and intangible matter. It may well be that you need to kiss a lot of frogs before you find your prince.

5. Do your deal on a contingent basis

This might be stating the obvious, but some management teams have been caught out in this area. Provided you are well-advised, it is usually possible to ensure that you are not exposed, or left holding the baby, if the deal falls over and fails to complete.

At the right time in the process, advisors are quite adept at securing some degree of cost underwriting from the vendor. These break-fee arrangements are useful in that they tend to provide some security and incentive to see a deal through.

6. Your strategy must be capable of being understood and implemented

Warren Buffett says if a plan can't fit on a side of A4 it can't be understood. Given that 80% of strategy is about implementation, what he's probably referring to is the difficulties businesses have of actually achieving their objectives without absolute clarity and understanding of strategy throughout the company.

Put another way, if you can't explain your strategy in an *elevator speech* (i.e. in twenty seconds), you probably can't explain it at all.

7. Take heed of the due diligence report

You will meet many managers who will have been scarred by the due diligence process. While due diligence is in many ways akin to a lifebuoy for the backers, it nonetheless shines a torch, of some intensity, into every corner of your business. Recognise that any management team's first instinct, when faced with criticism, is to deny it. Make sure it isn't you who is in denial.

Further, task a member of the management team with analysing the due diligence report and draw up a list of points to be addressed post-completion.

8. Your board must be effective

As Patrick Dunne of 3i wrote: "Bad boards destroy value." Directors must be individually and severally effective. The non-executive directors must add value and fit in as part of the team. An annual board calendar should be prepared and adhered to. Board papers should be circulated at least three working days before the meeting, and must contain information, not data. Really important performance indicators (e.g. cash forecasts and covenants), should be graphed and thus easily understood. The board agenda should focus upon key issues and decision making, and not allow endless waffle on merely exchanging information. Research shows conclusively that the most effective board meetings last between two and three hours. Communications between the board and fund providers must also be frequent, candid and well-managed.

9. Incentivise your important managers

Businesses are run by people. Retaining all of the potentially very valuable sweet equity amongst just the top team can be divisive. It may create an *us* and *them* mentality, which can be very counter-productive. Consider incentivising managers who are significant in the running of the business. Some companies have incentivised all employees, which is said to have had a very positive effect on the company's performance.

10. If it goes wrong, act fast and get outside help

Many MBOs/MBIs experience a drift from plan which invokes a recovery situation. If a company drifts from plan, remedial action must be taken very quickly. If analysis indicates this is not a one-off, but a recurring problem, then your survival is at stake. Recognise this and act accordingly. Frequently, the skills needed to reduce costs and generate cash are not available in the management team. You can train a rabbit to climb trees, but it's better to hire a squirrel! There are experienced individuals who specialise in these situations, and you should consider getting them on board to help you negotiate the choppy waters ahead.

11. The exit – seize the moment

It's highly unlikely that there will ever be a perfect time to exit. Inevitably, there will always be some clouds in view: a potential loss of a contract, a delisting, significant price increases in raw materials etc. However, if you have the opportunity of unloading your cargo of high-explosives (debt), and it is within the time-frame originally envisaged, then you will be well advised to take it. In short, *carpe diem*.

12. Be true to yourselves and the company

There will be several occasions where you face a moral maze. Whichever way you turn someone stands to lose. Advice may conflict and you will receive the most passionate advocacy from parties with different objectives. This can be graphically illustrated if you require a second, or third, round of fundraising. In these situations, do the right thing for the business as invariably this will, over differing timescales, benefit just about everyone involved with the company. Again, easier said than done, but it's the best compass. A great example is that of one serial entrepreneur I know: when trading was tough in the early stage of an MBO, he had a choice – pay the wages or the VAT. He got it right, he paid his employees!

Recommended reading

Directors' Dilemmas
Patrick Dunne
Kogan Page

Managing Board meetings
Patrick Dunne
Kogan Page

Venture Capital and Private Equity: A Practitioner's Manual
Graham Spooner
City and Financial

Go: An Airline Adventure
Barbara Cassani
Time Warner Book Group

The Art of War
Sun Tzu
Harper Collins

Acquisition
Nancy Hubbard
Palgrave Macmillan

Behind the Wheel at Chrysler
Doron P. Levin
Harcourt Brace

All these titles can be ordered through the Global Investor bookshop at:

www.global-investor.com

Alternatively call Global Investor on +44 (0)1730 233870

Appendix

Appendix

Taunton Cider

Key	1	2	3	4	5
	Very negative	Negative	Neutral	Positive	Very positive
	Unimportant	Significant	Crucial		

Criteria	Guide	Score (a) 1 to 5	Weighting (b) 1 to 3	Total (a) x (b)
Market				
Growth prospects	Based on recent history – can growth be forecasted with confidence?	4	3	12
Profitability	Are major players in the market making good profits?	4	2	8
Competitive intensity	Are industry profits stable? Threats in the future?	3	2	6
Route to market	Effective or a bottle-neck?	4	2	8
Gross margin level	Enough to go around or dog-eat-dog?	4	2	8
sub-total		19	11	42

Competitive position				
Market share	Relative market share against the market leader?	4	2	8
Market leadership	Are you a market leader or follower?	5	3	15
5-year trend in market share	Are you gaining or losing share?	5	3	15
New entrants	Are new entrants likely to destabalise the market?	3	2	6
Sub-total		17	10	44

Criteria	Guide	Score (a) 1 to 5	Weighting (b) 1 to 3	Total (a) x (b)
Marketing				
Brand strength	Do you have brands or commodities?	4	3	12
Media expenditure	How significant is your level of brand support?	4	2	8
Media consistency	Are you supporting your brands consisently or as and when it can be afforded?	4	1	4
Success with NPD	Do products introduced in the last few years account for a significant proportion of turnover?	5	2	10
Creative strength	Do you have well-known advertising campaigns?	5	2	10
Promotion	Do they build customer trial and/or loyalty or are they surrogate price reductions?	4	1	4
Image	Do you have a positive or tarnished image for your products?	4	1	4
Sub-total		30	12	52

Criteria	Guide	Score (a) 1 to 5	Weighting (b) 1 to 3	Total (a) x (b)
Customers				
Number of major customers	Do you have a good spread or are you heavily reliant on a small number?	3	3	9
Quality of relations	Are relations with major customers harmonious or strained?	4	3	12
Trading history	Is trading with your major customers well-established or relatively recent?	5	3	15
Chairman and CEO contacts	Do you have effective senior relationships or do you rely heavily on your sales management?	5	2	10
Knowledge of customers	Do you have a clean and well-used database or is it a fog?	4	2	8
Service levels	Do you meaningfully measure & understood these or are they guesstimated?	4	2	8
Customer satisfaction	Do you monitor these and what are complaints levels at a justifiable level?	4	3	12
Trade channel grip	Do you have a good level of 'control' of your routes to market?	4	3	12
Sub-total		33	21	86

Criteria	Guide	Score (a) 1 to 5	Weighting (b) 1 to 3	Total (a) x (b)
Production				
Supply chain	Is your supply chain robust or is it fragile?	3	2	6
Production efficiency	Does production run smoothly or is it running management ragged?	4	2	8
Capacity	Do you have adequate spare capacity (to meet your sales projections) or are you struggling to cope?	3	3	9
Cost of goods	Are these stable or increasing?	2	2	4
Raw materials availability	Do you have stable, predictable and a plentiful supply or is it difficult and unreliable?	2	2	4
Production sites – number	Do you operate from a single well-ordered site or do you have several disparate ones?	5	2	10
Production sites – quality	Are your production sites clean, environmentally sound and secure or a do you have a 'few issues'?	5	3	15
Quality of capital	Are your manufacturing assets modern and up to date or are they 'knackered'?	4	2	8
Sub-total		28	18	64

Distribution				
Costs	Are these costs small or substantial in relation to turnover?	4	2	8
In-house/ contracted-out	Do you add value by manufacturing in-house or should you be contracting-out?	4	1	4
Control of warehousing/ logistics	Do you have solid and professional control or is it frankly abdicated?	4	2	8
Sub-total		12	5	20

Criteria	Guide	Score (a) 1 to 5	Weighting (b) 1 to 3	Total (a) x (b)
IT and MIS				
Modernity	Do you have leading-edge technology and systems or quill pens and candles?	4	2	8
Website	Is this effective or really an electronic brochure?	0	2	0
Communications	Are you using modern technology to achieve good communications or are you still "printing off" emails?	5	3	15
Robustness of system	Are your systems effective and reliable or continually falling over?	4	2	8
Sub-total		13	9	31

People				
Principals preparedness	Do you understand and are you, individually and severally, prepared for the demands of an MBO/MBI?	5	3	15
Management track record	Are you a well-proven/settled team or newly-weds	5	3	15
Good board/ bad board	Is your board truly effective or a fuddled bureauocracy?	5	3	15
Absence rates	Are these above or below the industry norms?	5	2	10
Staff turnover	Do you have a history of stayers or more of a revolving door?	5	2	10
Equity involvement for senior management	Will all those managers, who will determine your success or failure, be adequately incentivised?	5	2	10
Sub-total		30	15	75

Criteria	Guide	Score (a) 1 to 5	Weighting (b) 1 to 3	Total (a) x (b)
Financial record				
5-year sales	Can you display consistent year on year growth or is it lumpy?	5	3	15
5-year margins	Are your margins trending up, flat or down?	5	2	10
Current net margin	10% is a good average. Above that is likely to be unsustainable. 5% is too low	4	3	12
Cash generation	This is your company's lifeblood - how strongly and consistently (seasonality) do you generate it?	4	3	12
Debtors	Do most major customers pay on time or do you have some taking over 90 days?	5	3	15
Creditors	Do you have a good payment record or have you stretched several too far?	3	3	9
Price increases	Can you still achieve these or are they a fading memory?	4	2	8
Sub-total		30	19	81

Financing				
Probable price	Are you likely to have to pay a high or low price to acquire your target company?	3	3	9
Senior debt availability	Do you have good asset backing against which to borrow funds?	5	3	15
Management equity	What is your appetite and ability to invest in this deal?	5	2	10
Ability to withstand due diligence	Will the business withstand its 'full structural survey' or are skeletons likely to be found?	4	3	12
Sub-total		17	11	46

Criteria	Guide	Score (a) 1 to 5	Weighting (b) 1 to 3	Total (a) x (b)
Exit prospects				
Possible trade buyers	Can you see trade buyers for your business in two or three years?	2	3	6
Flotation prospects	What are your prospects of achieving a flotation?	4	3	12
History of M&A in market	Have there been successful deals in your market in recent times or any notable failures?	2	3	6
Acquisitions	Will you need to acquire further businesses to achieve your business plan?			0
Sub-total		8	9	24

Other				
Cost savings potential	Is there low-hanging fruit to go after or has the business been 'too well-managed' already?	3	3	9
Ability to sell other products through distribution channels	Can you sell other goods and /or services in the future without expanding your sales resource?	3	1	3
Overseas potential	Do you have real potential here or is it more likely a recipe for bad debts and stock write-offs?	3	1	3
Vendor vacuum	Can you fill the vacuum left as your vendor withdraws?	5	3	15
Black hole possibility	Do you have any fears over a 'black-hole' being discovered beyond completion?	5	3	15
Sub-total		19	11	45

Index

A

B

C

G

H

I

J

K

L

R

S

T

Harriman House Titles

About Harriman House

Harriman House is a UK-based publisher which specialises in publishing books about money – how to make it, how to keep it, how to live with it, how to live without it. Harriman House offers an extensive catalogue of titles covering a variety of subjects, including: stock market investing, trading, personal finance, spread betting, and charting.

Some recent titles

Company valuation under IFRS
Interpreting and forecasting accounts using International Financial Reporting Standards
by Nick Antill and Kenneth Lee

International Financial Reporting Standards (IFRS) are now mandatory in Europe and are being adopted by other countries, including Australia. Written by practitioners for practitioners, this book addresses valuation from the viewpoint of the analyst, the investor and the corporate acquirer. It also explains the key differences between IFRS and US GAAP treatments of these issues, and their implications.

ISBN: 1897597525, Hardback, 416pp, 2005, Code: 20040, RRP: £39.99
www.harriman-house.com/ifrs

The Investor's Guide to Understanding Accounts

10 crunch questions to ask before investing in a company

by Robert Leach

The mission of this book is to explain to investors, with little or no accounting knowledge, what to look for in a company's accounts and how to interpret what is found, so that you have an accurate 'health check' on a company in ten simple steps. Robert Leach asks and then answers the ten questions which matter most, including: "does it make a profit?"; "Are there any hidden nasties?"; and "can I expect a reliable income?". He also looks at the techniques which companies sometimes use to flatter their accounts, and shows how accounts for companies in different sectors have to be looked at differently.

ISBN: 1897597274, Paperback, 246pp, 2004, Code: 15717, RRP: £19.99, www.harriman-house.com/accounts

Investing with Anthony Bolton

The anatomy of a stock market phenomenon

by Jonathan Davis

Who is the most successful investment manager in Britain? Arguments could rage forever, but no professional would dispute that Anthony Bolton of Fidelity is among the very best. £1,000 invested in his Special Situations fund at its launch in 1979 would today be worth more than £90,000.

Jonathan Davis looks at the way that Bolton goes about his business and analyses in detail the performance of the fund over the past 25 years. Anthony Bolton also gives his own personal account of the history of the fund and his stockpicking methods.

ISBN: 1897597509, Hardback, 120pp, 2004, Code: 20459, RRP: £12.99
www.harriman-house.com/anthonybolton

The eBay Book

Essential tips for buying and selling on eBay.co.uk

by David Belbin

In this book, David Belbin, a long time eBay user, explains how eBay.co.uk works and how to get the most out of it, whether you are a buyer or seller. Step-by-step, he takes you through the key features of the site, advises on bidding and selling tactics, explains how to minimise the fees you pay and why 'feedback' is so important. He explores the best ways to pay for goods, and what to do if your transactions go wrong. This hugely readable book also contains a wealth of case studies covering a wide variety of eBay users.

ISBN: 1897597436, Paperback, 160pp, 2004, Code: 19434, RRP: £9.99, www.harriman-house.com/ebay

The Global Investor Book of Investing Rules

Invaluable advice from 150 master investors

Edited by Philip Jenks and Stephen Eckett

For the first time, the tactics, strategies and insights relied on by 150 of the world's most respected financial experts are revealed in a concise, digestible form. Learn how you really make money in the markets from:

- fund managers of billion-pound equity funds
- economists from top business schools
- writers on leading financial newspapers
- traders in the options and futures markets

Each provides focused and practical rules on how to succeed in the market. Never before has so much quality advice been packed into a single book.

ISBN: 1897597215, Paperback, 502pp, 2002, Code: 14870, RRP: £19.99
www.harriman-house.com/rules

Alpesh B. Patel on Stock Futures

Strategies for profiting from stock futures

by Alpesh B. Patel

This book is for all stock traders who are interested in learning about one of the most efficient instruments for short-term trading: stock futures. It explains everything you need to know about stock futures, from basic characteristics to practical trading strategies. He highlights their special advantages, especially as a low-cost way of gaining exposure to non-UK equities, and shows how they can be employed to enhance returns and control portfolio risk.

ISBN: 1897597312, Paperback, 200pp, 2004, Code: 16176, Price: £19.99
www.harriman-house.com/stockfutures

The Beginner's Guide to Financial Spread Betting

Step-by-step instructions and winning strategies

by Michelle Baltazar

Spread betting was once the domain of institutional investors, city traders and high rollers. Not any more. You would now be hard-pressed to find any other form of trading that allows such a scale of return.

The aim of this book is to give you a basic understanding of how spread betting works, so that, with a little time and effort, you can find out how to turn a pauper's budget into a king's ransom.

However, an issue that should always be at the forefront of a novice spread better's mind is managing risk. As such, the secondary aim of this book is to explain the risks involved, and how to reduce them.

ISBN: 1897597355, Paperback, 140pp, 2004, Code: 16699, RRP: £12.99
www.harriman-house.com/spreadbetting

The Investor's Toolbox

How to use spread betting, CFDs, options, warrants and trackers to boost returns and reduce risk

by Peter Temple

This is the first book to set out all the choices open to investors. It explains how each of the derivative instruments works, the costs of dealing, the relationship to underlying share prices, and the risks involved. It shows how these instruments can be used alongside ordinary equity ownership, and provides examples of strategies designed to achieve specific ends.

In short, Peter Temple's guide is what ordinary equity investors have been waiting for; It will give you the confidence to step up from simple share ownership to the wider opportunities now available.

ISBN: 1897597258, Paperback, 272pp, 2003, Code: 15802, RRP: £21.99
www.harriman-house.com/toolbox

Marc Rivalland on Swing Trading

A guide to profitable short-term investing

by Marc Rivalland

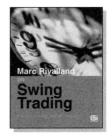

In this ground-breaking book, Marc Rivalland, author of 'The Trader' column in *Investors Chronicle*, shows how swing charts can be used to perfect market timing. Moreover, Marc reveals his hitherto secret modifications to Gann swing charts which make them even more effective for stock market traders. W. D. Gann said "a study of swings in active stocks will convince a man that he can make far greater profits in swings than in any other way of trading". With this book, you get Gann and more.

ISBN: 1897597193, Paperback, 214pp, 2002, Code: 14705, RRP: £39.99
www.harriman-house.com/swingtrading

If you would like to order any of these titles or request a copy of our catalogue, email us on enquiries@harriman-house.com, or call +44 (0)1730 233870. Our postal address is Harriman House, 43 Chapel Street, Petersfield, Hampshire, GU32 3DY, United Kingdom